DEEPER INTO GOD

DEEPER INTO GOD

A Handbook on
Spiritual Retreats

Brother Ramon SSF

Marshall Pickering

For

Mary Clare SLG, Spiritual Amma
Roland Walls CT, Spiritual Abba
in the love of Christ

Marshall Morgan and Scott
Marshall Pickering
3 Beggarwood Lane, Basingstoke, Hants RG23 7LP, UK

Copyright © 1987 Brother Ramon
First published in 1987 by Marshall Morgan and Scott
Publications Ltd
Part of the Marshall Pickering Holdings Group
A subsidiary of the Zondervan Corporation

2nd Impression

British Library Cataloguing in Publication Data

Ramon, *Brother, S.S.F.*
  Deeper into God.
  1. Christian life
  I. Title
  248.4   BV4501.2

  ISBN 0-551-01450-4

Text set in Linotron Plantin 11 on 12 point
by Input Typesetting Ltd., London SW19 8DR
Printed in Great Britain by The Guernsey Press Co. Ltd.,
Guernsey, Channel Islands.

Contents

Come yourselves apart
(Mark 6:31)

Come now yourselves apart and rest awhile;
    Weary, I know it, of the press and throng,
Wipe from your brow the sweat and dust of toil,
    And in My quiet strength again be strong.

Come now aside from all the world holds dear,
    For converse which the world has never known,
Alone with Me, and with My Father here,
    With Me and with My Father not alone.

Come, tell Me all that you have said and done,
    Your victories and failures, hopes and fears;
I know how hardly souls are wooed and won:
    My choicest wreaths are always wet with tears.

Come now and rest: the journey is too great,
    And you will faint beside the way and sink;
The Bread of Life is here for you to eat,
    And here for you the Wine of Love to drink.

Then, fresh from converse with your Lord, return
    And work till daylight softens into even;
The brief hours are not lost in which you learn
    More of your Master and His rest in Heaven.

Bishop E. H. Bickersteth

Introduction: What's it all about?

In a competitive world which emphasizes thrust, push, attack and getting in before one's opponent (all of which are particularly masculine traits*), the idea of retreat, passivity, openness and rest does not appeal. The religious world, particularly in the West, is no less 'worldly' than the secular in this respect, and the frenetic activity which accompanies much of our evangelism, administration and religious service has neither time nor place for retreat.

Perhaps as a corrective to all this, and certainly as a reaction to the reductionism in Christian theology and the devaluation of the life of prayer which has marked the last few decades, there has been a turning of the tide.

Christians who have adopted an activist stance in their work and witness are realizing their interior emptiness. Evangelism without spiritual roots, not sustained by the life of prayer, becomes verbosity. Dogmatic theology without the enthusiasm, the excitement and the experience of a baptism in the Holy Spirit, becomes an arid and boring scholasticism. Already busy Christians who engage in practical and committee work for relief agencies are increasingly aware of their spiritual poverty. And marching peacemakers and those engaged in protest against injustices and inequalities are suffering from a form of compassion fatigue.

In the midst of all this there has been growing an awareness, a desire, and an experience of retreat. It has many forms, but the withdrawal and passivity which it signifies is accompanied by an openness to the mystery of God, and an experience of resting passively in his love. The best analogies are those which are expressed in deep personal relationships: the child resting and feeding at its mother's

*It is appropriate to say here that the use of the masculine pronoun throughout this book, is generally to be taken in a generic, and not an exclusive, sense.

breast; the lover resting in the embrace of the beloved; and all the positive human relationships which bear the marks of mutual interior awareness.

The disciples were engaged in a demanding and compassionate work which was in the forefront of human need, and from which there was little respite. The demand engulfed the supply, the diseases threatened to paralyze the ministry of the healers. So in the face of such a situation, Jesus said: 'Come away by yourselves to a lonely place, and rest a while.'[1]

This book sets out to repeat the pattern of Jesus in the school of discipleship. When he called his disciples into retreat it was for the sake of a renewal of the divine life within them. There was an indispensable mystical element in which his divine life was renewed in their lives and ministries, and there was an anointing of the Holy Spirit in which the mystery of God's loving indwelling was renewed and communicated.

These chapters constitute a practical guide to the making of a retreat, and 'how to do it' is the guiding principle. But if it is to be really practical there must be some clear and basic awareness of what we are about. It is not enough to let go the ordinary routines of life and enter into some kind of solitude or desert – that would be the way to madness, or to another ego trip which feeds a negative narcissism. The purpose of a retreat is to go deeper into God, to be embraced by the divine mystery that sustains the whole fabric of the created order. This mystery is manifested in the beauty and pattern of the world, and in the compassion which led to the redemption of the world by our Lord Jesus Christ.

Our first task then is one of *Definition*. We shall define what is meant by a spiritual retreat, examine the biblical roots of wilderness, vision and revelation in the living experience of the Bible, and trace the flowering of such spirituality and prayer in the lives and words of the Desert Fathers who flourished in the first few centuries after the New Testament. And in the course of definition we shall note what some people say about their experience of retreat.

Secondly we shall proceed to the task of *Application*. That is, we shall take the insights and principles of the first section and apply them to our own particular situation. This will be a practical section which will deal with the methods and 'know-how' of meditation, prayer, the use of scripture, silence and solitude, and the types of individual and corporate retreats which are possible. This leads to a consideration of forms of commitment to a gospel life which are implicit in the making of a retreat.All the practical information involved in the preparation and conduct of oneself in retreat will be included in this section, as well as advice and warnings which are necessary in some forms of retreat.

The last section, *Pilgrimage*, describes the making of a retreat as a continuing journey into the depths of oneself and into the mystery of God. It is both a personal and a corporate journey, and the chapters in that last section lead into an ever-deepening awareness of the joy and the pain involved in such a spiritual pilgrimage. It is a life-long quest, and retreat is only part of it, but to the Christian who avails himself of the opportunity, the making of a retreat is an invaluable progressive experience.

In my own pilgrimage I began by making my daily times of prayer and Bible reading periods of retreat into God. I then 'took off' with forms of meditation and prayer which involved simple disciplines and techniques of meditative prayer.[2] This led to setting aside a week, and then a fortnight alone, in a caravan and a loaned cottage. I have also done this with a friend, using the methods and disciplines of prayer which I had already practised alone. Then as I went deeper into God, I was privileged to be granted two six-month periods of solitude. And still the pilgrimage goes on.

This book, therefore, is to initiate the reader into the dimension of retreat and pilgrimage in which every step leads to a fuller and deeper experience of the Holy Spirit. Life in God is meant to be an *experienced* life, leading to an awareness of the divine presence as well as the divine absence. Retreat opens out into that experiential dimension in which one learns not only with the mind, but also in the heart, the powerful meaning of the Gospel of death and resurrection.

There are included forms and patterns of prayers and

meditations which you may use on an unconducted retreat, but scripture and solitude in the context of openness to God should be at the heart of your retreat, and the substance of this book, theological and practical, will help you on the way.

Brother Ramon SSF,
The Society of St Francis,
Glasshampton Monastery,
Worcester.

References

1 Mark 6:31.
2 See Brother Ramon SSF, *A Hidden Fire*, Part II., (Basingstoke: Marshall Pickering), pp. 63ff. Hereafter abbreviated *HF*.

PART I: DEFINITION

Biblical and Theological Basis

1: The Idea of a Retreat

A First Glimpse

Taking the 1.10 p.m. train from Waterloo brings you to the lovely Dorset town of Sherborne at about 3.25 p.m. The imposing tower of the abbey rises before you just half a mile from the station, but before you have time to reflect upon it, you see a brown-habited friar taking the suitcase of a fellow he seems to know, putting it into the boot of the friary car, and looking around for the other two passengers who are expected for the friary retreat.

You make yourself known, there are smiles, introductions, and you are whisked away through the Dorset countryside to the tiny hamlet of Hilfield, with its small church, a few scattered farmhouses, and surrounding fields populated with sheep, cattle, deer and pheasants. The journey takes about half an hour and you soon find yourself in the grounds of the friary. Getting out of the car you are conducted, with your fellow-passengers who are also retreatants, past the chapel and recreation room, past Leo House and Bernard House to the Guesthouse where you are settled into a warm, single room by the friendly Guestbrother who will look after your needs during the days of retreat.

This retreat is not silent, though there is a sharing of the 'greater silence' of the friary from 9.30 p.m. to 9.00 a.m. and participation in the chapel services and meditation periods following. The theme of the retreat is *Healing* in its spiritual, physical, personal and communal aspects. The retreat conductor gives retreat addresses and is available for personal interviews during the (otherwise) free afternoon periods. There is a daily eucharist and the friary meals are communal. At any given meal the retreatant may have a wayfarer on one side and a bishop on the other – both are as welcome as the retreatant! There may be arrangements for the retreatants to eat apart from the rest of the community, and in silence.

There is a corporate sharing as well as space and time for deep personal reflection, with the possibility of sharing and silence as the retreatant requires. The afternoon walks alone are as important as the ministry and fellowship within the friary, and food and sleep in the context of a religious house are all part of the week's retreat. The conversations and friendships made all become part of what can be an exhilarating experience of one's first retreat.

A Second Glimpse

From the outset there is a sense of pilgrimage. Having arrived in Birmingham (or Worcester), you get the X93 coach which runs through the village of Shrawley, Worcestershire, alighting at Glazenbridge. A rough track runs up for three-quarters of a mile to the gate of St Mary at the Cross Monastery, known as Glasshampton.[1] Whereas the friary at Hilfield is active and busy with brothers, guests, members of St Francis' House, long term residents, wayfarers and perhaps campers and school groups, Glasshampton is the house of prayer for the Society of St Francis, and the atmosphere is appropriately quiet. There are five single guest rooms and the retreatant expects to remain in comparative (or complete) silence. Meals are silent (save for tea), and though there are necessary conversations in the kitchen and during work periods, the greater part of the monastery is kept quiet, with the emphasis on prayer, silence and manual work. Having said that, I have been interrupted during the writing of this page by cattle bursting the monastery fence, and have spent half an hour with the other friars getting them back into their appropriate field!

The retreatant will spend his time sharing in the daily round of worship, study and (if he desires) manual work. Guidance and counselling on a personal basis may be part of the retreat. But the emphasis at Glasshampton will be on silence and solitude, within and outside the monastery grounds. 'Being available to God' is the right attitude, with

14

no prepared agenda, but with heart and mind open to the interior movement of the Holy Spirit, with the possibility of spiritual guidance where necessary. Obviously, the 'first-time' retreatant will not be able to follow so stringent a procedure – but we shall talk later about the different types of retreat in their own context.

The two terms we use commonly for time out of our ordinary lives indicate what retreats are about – the one is *vacation*, and the other *holiday*. The word *vacation* indicates an open and empty space, an arena of silence and stillness for God to work, a vacating of oneself from the ordinary and legitimate pursuits of daily work, to spend time with God. It also means a place of interior emptiness in which to welcome the Lord, and in which his interior indwelling may be experienced without distraction.

The word *holiday* indicates that the time thus spent is not vacuity, a negative vacuum which could be dangerous, but rather a sanctifying, a redeeming of the time. Holiday becomes *holy-day* in which holiness suffuses the period of retreat, and in which God initiates his movement of love for the believer, and in which the heart reaches out in response to God.

Variations on the theme

These are but two glimpses of quite different kinds of retreat within our own Franciscan Order, and there are many more in different kinds of monasteries, friaries and retreat houses. I shall be referring to the different kinds of retreat, but it is already evident that there are great potentialities for personal and corporal growth, both psychologically and spiritually, if the regular practice of 'making a retreat' becomes part of the joy and discipline of one's Christian life.

Of course you don't have to 'beat a retreat' to some monastic house or join some pious and snooty group who specialize in such things (and they do exist!). Jesus went into the desert, and in the biblical tradition the prophets obeyed the interior call of God to go into the wilderness. The Desert Fathers and the Celtic monks were just as spontaneous, for when the Lord said 'Come!' they came;

and when the Lord said 'Go!' they went! There are stories of the Celtic monks of Ireland and Wales in which the brother would get into a small boat, throw away the oars and say in effect: 'Well Lord, take me where you want me.' There is an element of the fool in the early monastic traditions which follow the biblical pattern, and I shall be talking about that later. The point I'm making here is that the retreat is *into God*, and God is wherever he calls you, and wherever you call upon him. Of course the Lord speaks through people, through corporate community life, especially when the community is gathered around prayer and scripture. But whenever the Lord gave new, epoch-making revelation, it was usually in the context of wilderness, desert, mountain and retreat. The geographical setting often reflected the interior solitude, and out of such a solitary and wilderness confrontation emerged the divine word of revelation for a whole people. Sometimes the word came in the desert, under the stars with Abraham; sometimes within the mysterious conflict and struggle of wrestling Jacob; sometimes at the burning bush with Moses, and sometimes in domestic quietness with the young Hebrew peasant woman, Mary. But the idea of *retreat* is always there, within the silence and interiority of the soul, and the true response was always from a humble and obedient heart, as in Mary's response to Gabriel's message: 'Behold, I am the handmaid of the Lord; let it be to me according to your word.'[2]

If you take this book seriously and begin to order your life in spending time and making space for God, then the pattern of prayer will lead you into a more contemplative orientation. The positive spiritual, psychical and physical results will make you a better human being, combining the blessings which St Paul envisages in his advice to Timothy, his son in the faith: 'Train yourself in godliness; for while bodily training is of some value, godliness is of value in every way, as it holds promise for the present life and also for the life to come.'[3]

References

1 The story of Glasshampton, its conversion from former
  stables, and the story of Fr William, its founder, is

told in *William of Glasshampton*, by Geoffrey Curtis CR,
(SPCK).
2 Luke 1:38.
3 I Tim. 4:8.

2: The Biblical Background

A. Old Testament Roots

Remarkable things happen when confronted with scripture in retreat. There are times when one's heart and mind are set upon seeking God, when one has come apart from the world and from the frenetic activity of daily necessities, that a stillness of mind and body become possible. In such a situation, scripture can yield some of its treasures. Here is the marvel of inspiration. It is not that there is some mechanical magical power within the words, but that in personal confrontation and dialogue with scripture, truth and life leap out of the pages, and the same Spirit who inspired the prophets and apostles is here and now at work in the reader's heart. For 'is not my word like fire, says the Lord, and like a hammer which breaks the rock in pieces.'[1]

Of course we are not all initiators of new religious movements or revivals – most of us do not find ourselves at the source of an epoch in God's dealings with mankind and we are not vouchsafed such an immediate and mind-blowing revelation of God that begins a new chapter in spiritual history. Nevertheless, the basic and primordial stories of revelation in scripture constitute a kind of paradigm or analogy of God's ways with all his people. In Adam and Eve is told the story of the fall of every man and woman. As Joseph dreams his dreams, descends into the pit, is sold into slavery, languishes in prison and begins his miraculous ascent to the right hand of the sovereign, so we are caught up in the amazing providential acts of God. We are carried through pain and darkness, dreaming and reflection, suffering and trial, to the glory of sharing in Christ's passion and resurrection.

Prerequisites to Vision

There are certain prerequisites to vision which are exemplified in the biblical pattern. Whenever there occurs one of the peak experiences of men and women of God in scripture there is a call to retreat, a period of reflection, a pattern of certain passive receptivity. This may take the form of world-weariness and bankruptcy, a feeling of unworthiness and deep repentance, an experience of being smitten by the terrifying holiness of God, or a quiet reflection or curiosity as the man or woman is drawn into the place of vision. But certainly there is that element of preparedness, expectancy or retreat. There are variations in the pattern because God deals with us differently, but the pattern begins in the secret places of the soul. This may not always be explicit, but perusal of the text will give clues to the persistence of this pattern. For instance, it seems in the story of the conversion of Saul of Tarsus on the Damascus road that he was suddenly apprehended by the risen Christ with no previous warning, by what he calls a heavenly vision.[2]

But the Holy Spirit did not *begin* his work on the Damascus Road. There was a long period of preparation, when the soil was made ready, the seed was planted and the sunshine and rain of God's providential growth brought Saul to the place where he seemed to be suddenly seized, and when he surrendered tremblingly and eventually joyfully, to the risen Christ. He spent hours of reflective retreat not only in Arabia after his conversion, but also in solitude before his conversion. In the simple but powerful cartoon picture illustrating Acts 8:1 in the *Good News Bible*, Saul is depicted looking on at the stoning of Stephen. The caption runs: 'And Saul approved of his murder.' The *fact* that he stands there saying and doing nothing to help or vindicate Stephen indicates approval. But the *manner* in which he stands indicates perplexity, wonder and profound disturbance in the face of such Christlike saintliness in Stephen's martyrdom: 'And as they were stoning Stephen, he prayed, "Lord Jesus, receive my spirit." And he knelt down and cried with a loud voice, "Lord, do not hold this sin against them." And when he had said this, he fell asleep.'[3] The point here, as in the following Old Testament passages, is that before God acts overtly, and prior to any public or recognized movement or decision on man's part, there is the interior movement of God's Holy Spirit. This often involves the calling aside to a quiet state of mind in a solitary geographical location, the better to hear, feel and recognize the word and will of God.

Jacob, fugitive at Bethel (Genesis 28:10–17)

In this passage, Jacob is a homeless fugitive, negatively fleeing from his hostile brother Esau, and positively seeking a home and a wife. Providentially, the Lord brought him at sunset, between Beersheba and Haran, to a holy place where he lay down, his head resting upon a stone. The guidance and preparedness for dream and vision were here entirely to do with the divine initiative, and Jacob co-operated, unconscious of the implications. The glory of confrontating Yahweh in such a place and at such a time was overwhelming, for in this story there is not only the communication between earth and heaven by the heavenly stairway, but the terrifying and awesome vision of Yahweh himself. The content of the communication is full of promise and blessing, but the manner of the meeting is numinous and full of the mysterious and tremendous quality of awe, which is the unutterable power and glory of the living God.

Then Jacob woke and cried out in trembling wonder: ' "Surely the Lord is in this place; and I did not know it." And he was afraid and said, "How awesome is this place! This is none other than the house of God, and this is the gate of heaven." ' In that bleak wilderness God revealed to Jacob that there was commerce with heaven. And this 'ladder of Jacob' prefigured the relationship between God and man which was manifested in its fulness in the mediating cross of Christ:

As Jacob with travel was weary one day,
At night on a stone for a pillow he lay;
He saw in a vision a ladder so high,
That its foot was on earth and its top in the sky:
Alleluya to Jesus, who died on the tree,
And has raised up a ladder of mercy for me.[4]

Jacob wrestling with the Angel (Genesis 32:22–32)

The story of Jacob is one of continuing conversion. And the means by which the Lord brought this about was by meeting him in the wilderness, the solitary place, at night, and alone. The second passage is one which emphasizes the importance of such a context. It is many years later, but 'the Hound of Heaven' is still on his track, and now, quite literally, will not let him go. The scene is set when Jacob, fleeing from the imagined wrath of Esau, sends on companies of his servants and cattle, followed by his wives and children, across the river Jabbok, until he is left alone. In the darkness and solitude of that wilderness he is apprehended by a powerful figure who lays hold on him, hand to hand, face to face, limb to limb, and wrestles with him mightily throughout the night.

The combat is full of agonizing struggle and pain. No hold is barred, and Jacob feels the strength draining from his body. Nor is that all. The encounter is not only physical and mental, but spiritual. This is no mere man wrestling with him, but the Angel of the Lord – and in Old Testament reckoning that is a synonym for God himself. Through the darkness there is a confession of self-despair, a cry for spiritual wisdom, and a change of identity and character is involved, as Jacob cries out as the day is breaking: 'Who are you . . . what is your name. . . ?'

I have read some very powerful and beautiful expositions of this passage,[5] but none can compare with the hymn of Charles Wesley on the theme of Wrestling Jacob. There are times now when I sing it quietly in prayer, in the awareness of God's loving presence:

> Come, O thou Traveller unknown
>   Whom still I hold, but cannot see;
> My company before is gone,
>   And I am left alone with thee;
> With thee all night I mean to stay
> And wrestle till the break of day.
>
> I need not tell thee who I am,
>   My misery and sin declare;
> Thyself hast called me by my name,

Look on thy hands and read it there:
But who, I ask thee, who art thou?
Tell me thy name, and tell me now.

In vain thou strugglest to get free;
    I never will unloose my hold:
Art thou the Man that died for me?
    The secret of thy love unfold:
Wrestling, I will not let thee go
Till I thy name, thy nature know.

Yield to me now, for I am weak,
    But confident, in self-despair;
Speak to my heart, in blessings speak,
    Be conquered by my instant prayer:
Speak, or thou never hence shalt move,
And tell me if thy name is Love.

'Tis Love, 'tis Love! Thou diedst for me!
    I hear thy whisper in my heart;
The morning breaks, the shadows flee,
    Pure, universal Love thou art:
To me, to all, thy mercies move;
Thy nature and thy name is Love.[6]

There are twelve stanzas in all – all recorded in the *Methodist Hymn Book*, and wedded to the tune *David's Harp*. They may be read and sung as a personal or group contemplative exercise, followed by a half hour's silence. It is remarkable the way in which an ancient Old Testament passage like this can portray and communicate sublime, existential truth, challenging, piercing and blessing as it does. The theme continues in Jacob's family.

Joseph: Beloved, Rejected, Exalted (Genesis 37: 39–45)
The Joseph cycle of stories is one filled with dreams and visions, and one in which Joseph is portayed as a young man and a mature one, full of the wisdom and discernment which come from long and silent contemplation in God. His early years are full of the contemplative dreams which the divine wisdom communicates to him. They are dreams of earth and of heaven, of the idyllic pastoral scenes of

cornfields and golden grain, and of the wide expanse of heaven studded with sun, moon and stars.

This world of dream and vision was not merely the product of Joseph's fertile imagination. He spent much time meditating in the cornfields and under the night sky. Contemplative foundations were well laid in his young life, so that he would have spiritual reserves to carry him through the dark valleys of humiliation and loneliness. Divine wisdom was born within him so that he would be able to communicate the fruits of his contemplation to those who stood in dire need of his life of prayer and communion with God.

One only has to read the cycle of stories to realize that Joseph's communion with God was both chosen and coerced, in the sense that he had a spontaneous love for God, and was cast upon God in utter loneliness and abandonment. There were fearful moments of the apprehension of death in the pit when his brothers left him to die; there were many hours of weariness and approaching exhaustion as he was led away in the slave train to Egypt, and there were years of seemingly meaningless waiting in Pharaoh's prison, enduring an undeserved punishment.

It was precisely because Joseph was such a man of mystical prayer and contemplative imagination that the seeds of glory could be planted within his young heart. It was because he had applied himself in discipline as well as responded in spontaneity that God could prepare him and trust him with sorrow, pain, loneliness, rejection and seeming abandonment. The mysterious providence of God was always at work, and in retrospect Joseph was able to look back over a patchwork life of experiences and say: 'God sent me before you to preserve for you a remnant . . . so it was not you who sent me here, but God.' And to his brothers who had betrayed, sold, and lied about him all those years, he said; 'You meant evil against me, but God meant it for good, to bring it about that many people should be kept alive, as they are today.' This was the reward of the patient and contemplative soul. As St Paul would have commented: 'We know that in everything God works for good with those who love him, who are called according to his purpose.'[7]

23

Joseph's early days of retreat were voluntary. He revelled in his dreams and spent many hours in solitude in the pastoral context of nomadic life. But his later experience was one of enforced retreat from the natural world which he loved, and in exile from family and home. The whole experience of voluntary and enforced retreat stood Joseph in good stead when he was called upon to give mature judgments before Pharaoh in the land of Egypt. The basis of sound action is rooted in rich contemplative soil, and contemplative personal integrity led to corporate blessing in the experience of the patriarch Joseph.

Moses and the Burning Bush (Exodus 3:1–18)

Right from his birth, Moses was a man set apart for God. He was constantly drawn into an awareness of the divine presence and glory, so that 'the LORD would speak to Moses face to face as a man speaks to his friend.' Later in his life as a leader of Israel he often withdrew into the wilderness, sometimes into the specially pitched Tent of the Presence away from the camp, and sometimes the call would sound from the holy mountain. But the primary thing was not retreat away *from* the people but retreat *into* God, to gaze upon the unutterable glory, and reflect its radiance.

There are two particular incidents in the life of Moses which indicate both the initiative of God and the contemplative waiting upon God on the part of his servant. The first concerns the call of Moses in the passage about the burning bush.

Years had passed since Moses had fled from Egypt. He was living a pastoral life, looking after Jethro's sheep in the lonely pasture-land under the shadow of mount Horeb. Here were the simple conditions of revelation: a man in solitude, with openness of heart, having retreated from the pomp and politics of Egyptian society. The place was right, the time was right, the man was right. And suddenly Moses caught sight of the common bush aflame with God.

A burning bush was a common enough sight in that sun-scorched place, but this bush kept on burning. It had the mysterious drawing power of holiness and revelation, and as soon as Moses' curiosity was aroused, he was suddenly exposed to the mystery and burning of God's holiness. 'Moses, Moses!' came the call. 'Here am I,' was the trembling answer. 'Do not come near;' said the Lord, 'put off your sandals from your feet, for the place on which you are standing is holy ground.' Moses obeyed, listened with amazement as God revealed himself as the great God of Israel, and he covered his face with awe and perplexity.

This was the pattern of wilderness revelation. Only here would God speak with Moses face to face, and deliver such a charge and command such an obedience. In this place of solitude and holiness Moses' life was transformed, and he became the man to lead the people of God out of slavery into freedom. It could have been said that Moses' flight from the Egyptian court was a fleeing from his social and political responsibilities, a retreat into the wilderness of irrelevance and selfish piety. But that's where the *presence* was, and that's where the *action* was! God's ways are not our ways.

Moses on Mount Sinai (Exodus 33:18–23; 34:29–35)

If we move from Horeb to Sinai, we shall find a further development in the unfolding vocation of Moses. He is now the leader of ancient Israel, and has need of further revelation and further vision. It was not just a matter of the legal commandments on letters of stone being given him, but of the transformation of his very being. There is a continual process of purgation and illumination taking place. Body, mind and spirit are caught up in the sanctifying process.

In a moment of great desire and daring Moses makes a request which God himself has put into his heart: 'I pray you, show me your glory. . . ' God makes it clear to him that no man can gaze upon his unutterable glory and remain alive. This profound sense of God's dazzling glory being too devastating for our poor mortality to bear is reflected in the later Christian tradition: '. . . the blessed and only Sovereign, the King of kings and Lord of lords, who alone has immortality and dwells in unapproachable light, whom no man has ever seen or can see. . .'[8]

Responding to Moses' request, yet guarding his own ineffable mystery, the Lord tells him that he will place him

25

within the cleft of a rock for safety, and then his goodness, his mercy and his glory shall pass by. The cleft of the rock would be covered by the hand of the Lord, for such exposure would otherwise be sufficient to threaten his finitude and consume him. 'Then I will take away my hand, and you shall see my back,' says the Lord, 'but my face shall not be seen.'

Along with all this communication of the divine presence is the fact that God makes himself known to Moses by proclaiming his holy name *Yahweh*. This name was so sacred that in the later history of the people of God it was never spoken. This is reflected in the Authorized and Revised Standard Versions of the bible when the sacred name is always replaced in the translation by the words The LORD in capital letters. Although God told Moses that no man was able to look upon the divine Face and live, yet Moses is spoken of as the patriarch who spoke with God face to face. And this divine communication and communion took place primarily in the desert and upon the holy mountain. The biblical roots of retreat are found in such experiences as this in the holy men of old. Only in such places of solitude and retreat could exposure to God at such a level take place, and only in such confrontation and communion could Moses receive the transfiguring power and interior strength to lead the people of God out of slavery into freedom and the land of liberty.

The accusation is sometimes made that retreat is running away from the responsibilities and perplexities of the real and demanding world. There is, of course, an element of turning away in retreat, but the basic meaning of retreat is an exploration into the regenerating and transfiguring glory of God. The consequences of such retreat are found in the later verses of the chapter we have been following.[9] It's worth looking them up!

Moses spent a prolonged period, fasting, upon the holy mountain, then made the descent from Sinai, altogether unconscious of the fact that his face shone with the radiance of his communion with God. Both Aaron and the people were afraid when they saw this radiance, and the result was that Moses had to veil his face, for the glory was too much for the people to gaze upon. St Paul marvels at the glory which shone from Moses' face, and says that even such splendour as that cannot compare with the indwelling presence and glory of the Holy Spirit in the life of the believer.[10] Then he goes on to say: 'And we all, with unveiled face, beholding the glory of the Lord, are being changed into his likeness from one degree of glory to another; for this comes from the Lord who is the Spirit.'[11]

The effect of Moses' retreat into God in the wilderness and upon the holy mountain was that the radiance of God's splendour was dispersed and shared among the people of God. This is a sharing of the fruits of contemplation. St Seraphim the 19th century Russian staretz (elder) and hermit testifies that when the Spirit of God descends upon a man and overshadows him with the fulness of his outpouring, then his soul overflows with a joy not to be described, for the Holy Spirit turns to joy whatever he touches, and imparts inward peace. 'Acquire inward peace,' he writes, 'and thousands around you will find their salvation.' Certainly, if Moses had not obeyed the inward prompting of the Holy Spirit to retreat into the desert or up onto the mountain height, he would never have been the instrument of God's revelation to his ancient people and to the world.

The glory that Moses beheld both at the burning bush and upon the mountain hidden in the cleft of the rock, was the objective, transcendent glory of the God who is high and lifted up. But it was also the subjective and hidden glory that transfigured his inner life, suffused his being, and overflowed in the radiance of light that shone in his very flesh. The word *transfiguration* is a literal rendering of the Greek *metamorphosis* which is the New Testament word.[12] It indicates not merely a moral change, but an irradiation of the whole of one's being, a suffusion by the Holy Spirit, a transformation of the human into the divine, mirroring in our humanity the image of God.

Moses' experience was not an isolated one. When the protomartyr Stephen stood before the religiously bigoted members of the Sanhedrin, he bore courageous witness to his Lord. The exciting description of his trial is one of a man possessed by the power of the Holy Spirit. They could not withstand his words of wisdom, and even as they looked upon him, his face appeared to them as the face of an angel. After he had rehearsed before them the great story of Israel's salvation-history, they were so angered, convicted and desperately violent that they stopped their ears and rushed upon him to stone and lynch him. Their anger broke upon him as he lifted his contemplative gaze and proclaimed: 'Behold, I see the heavens opened, and the Son of Man standing at the right hand of God.'[13] So freely forgiving his murderers, he yielded his spirit to the Lord.

The transfiguration experiences of Moses in the Old Testament and of Stephen in the New Testament are of a similar nature to that of the Transfiguration of Jesus to which we shall refer later.

Elijah in Retreat

I have referred to retreat in terms of discipline and choice. The believer may take off into the desert to deepen his life of prayer, or as a rest from the struggles and stresses of daily life – a time of physical, mental and spiritual renewal. But in the experience of the great prophet Elijah we discover another element. On the one hand his desert experience is the result of an imperative word from the Lord: 'Depart from here . . . and hide yourself by the brook Cherith. . . ' There is no choice about it – it is a command to be obeyed. On the other hand, some years later, Elijah takes off into the desert for quite a different reason. The fearless and powerful Hebrew prophet is scared out of his wits by the threat of the heathen Queen, Jezebel, and he beats a hasty retreat to the wilderness of Beer-sheba, and then a further day's journey alone into the deeper desert. Both forms of retreat are contained within the wider plan of God, though Elijah did not know that at the time.

Elijah at Cherith: Drought and Refreshment (I Kings 17:1–7)

The prophet Elijah appears suddenly in Israel's history, and eventually disappears quite as suddenly, though remarkably.[14] Without obvious or explicit preparation he bursts in upon the heathen and royal scene, announcing to King Ahab the powerful and unpalatable word of the Lord: 'As the Lord the God of Israel lives, before whom I stand, there shall be neither dew nor rain these years, except by my word.'

As a result of such a threatening prophetic word, the Lord drives him into the desert, and throughout the early days of drought and famine he is miraculously sustained with food and water at the brook Cherith which runs into the Jordan. Here begins a time of seclusion and hiddenness in the experience of Elijah which really continued his early training in wilderness and solitude, for he was the prototype of John the Baptist.[15] This Cherith solitude led to a sojourn with the widow woman of Zarepath, filling up three years of retreat until he was to meet Ahab again.

It is a mistake to think of the prophets of Israel displaying a 'prophetic religion' which encapsulated and communicated the objective word of Yahweh, devoid of mystical experience. One cannot separate such prophetic faith from mystical experience in the history of Israel, for the prophetic ministry was sustained by an inward mystical indwelling in which transcendence and immanence met in an overwhelming experience of the living God, both high and lifted up and yet intimately interior. Without such inward and mystical indwelling, none of the prophets could have been sustained, although the deepest and most interior experiential understanding of God was to be made known in the new covenant in Christ. The great prophets glimpsed such inward truth and prophesied of its fulness, but it was only in the coming of the Pentecostal Spirit that the fulness was to be experienced.[16]

The experience of Elijah was both prophetic and mystical – the mystical undergirding of his prophetic ministry was indispensable, and it was in the wilderness that he learned his own inadequacy, and his ultimate dependence upon God. God called him apart in order to communicate his word to Elijah, to initiate new spiritual experience and to deepen his faith. During these years of drought and famine he was also protected in retreat from the violent hands of Ahab and Jezebel, and even though he was prohibited from public ministry he was able to mediate the tenderness of God to the widow woman in sustaining her life and restoring miraculously the life of her only son. Her witness to the validity of Elijah's desert experience is evident: 'Now

I know that you are a man of God, and that the word of the Lord in your mouth is truth.'[17]

Don't be discouraged if you feel that your experience of retreat cannot attain to such high motives as 'the love of God alone'. Loving service, renewal, refreshment and growth in discipleship may be humbler motives, but it is not up to us to define motivation too clearly. The first shall be last and the last first, and those who think their feet to be planted on the high road of holiness may be deluded. And those who feel that they are on the lowly path of humble service may truly be just beneath the summit of the mount. 'Let any one who thinks that he stands take heed lest he fall.'[18]

So if you feel the gentle constraint of love to move into retreat, that's alright. But if you feel driven by circumstances, drawn by longing, encouraged by weakness, or even moved by sanctified curiosity – that's alright too. There are many reasons for movement into retreat as you see from Elijah's experience. But let us now see how human fear and weakness can serve the wider purposes of God's love.

Elijah at Horeb: Fear, Flight and Confrontation (I Kings 19:1–13)

One would not ordinarily think of a spiritual retreat in a monastic house as the venue for someone who is running away from his enemies, fears, frustrations or judgment! But there are times from our side, when we receive people into the hospitality of our Society who have retreated into a house of prayer, friary or monastery because they are full of fears in the world outside. It may be that they feel alienated by the technological age or by the bureaucratic and political scene. Sometimes they have come to the edge of a mental precipice in their university examinations, have sexual or drug problems or are faced by a moral or domestic dilemma. Retreat, for these people, seems to be the negative thing that other people have always suspected it might be. Their retreat is interpreted as running away, a retreat and flight from confrontation with themselves, their fears and their enemies. And of course, this may indeed be the case.

30

But it may also be a good thing! In Elijah's experience, the only thing open to him seemed to be flight. There is a certain ambivalence in some biblical advice, depending on the circumstances. On the one hand we read: 'Resist the devil and he will flee from you . . . ' but on the other: 'flee youthful lusts which war against the soul. . . '[19] Do you *stand* – or do you *run*? Well it all depends. Elijah ran. And yet, although we may judge him morally wrong, humanly weak, mentally a coward, it was the only thing he could do. He was spiritually drained, mentally maimed and physically exhausted by the events on Mount Carmel. And as the text shows, he was disillusioned with himself and utterly dejected.

It is easy to detect such feelings in ourselves. This may surprise you, but those of us who are 'on the inside' of friary or monastery walls feel that Elijah's experience is often reflected in our own – quite apart from those sections of our poor humanity who come to us for help of different kinds. It is not difficult to discover the disillusioned and exhausted Elijah in the monk or nun, in the guest or retreatant, in the lodger, wayfarer, or priest who people our convents, friaries, monasteries and retreat houses.

When Elijah sunk down exhausted and made his complaint to the Lord he discovered he was wrong on three counts. He ran to the furthest confines of Ahab and Jezebel's jurisdiction, and leaving his servant at the boundary of the cultivated land he goes deeper into the wilderness. There he collapses under a broom tree and requests his death:

> It is enough, now, O Lord,
> take away my life;
> for I am no better than my fathers.

But it was not enough. The Lord had much for him to do. His life was never to be taken away, for the Lord had appointed a chariot of fire. And certainly he was better than his fathers. We know nothing of them, but Elijah inspired the greatest of men, John the Baptist, and appeared with our Lord on the holy mount of Transfiguration. How wrong you were, Elijah. You certainly needed a retreat!

What a pattern for retreat Elijah becomes for us – in spite of the fact that he retreated negatively into the wilderness for all the wrong reasons, and in spite of the fact that we would easily have judged his behaviour reprehensible. The Lord's plan and pattern for us is often born of human failure. Just when we are exhausted, drained and disillusioned – just when we have only enough energy to make that final spurt away from God in negative retreat – then that becomes the place of God's appointing. Sometimes it is under a broom tree in the wilderness; sometimes, like Jonah, it is in the belly of a great fish. And sometimes it is in Glasshampton monastery!

The Still, Small Voice of Calm

It is at this point that we find the Lord dealing lovingly, tenderly with his exhausted and disillusioned servant. He is fed, refreshed and sustained by angelic ministry, and then the divine tenderness gently unfolds as the Lord leads him to Horeb, the mount of God.

The 'forty days and forty nights' associated with Moses and with Jesus are found here – a time of solitude, prayer and contemplation.[20] Whereas Moses was hidden in the cleft of the rock, Elijah hides his face in his mantle, at the mouth of a cave, and now begins the series of events which herald a confrontation with God – what in Old Testament theology is called a *theophany*, literally a manifestation of God.[21]

There is a pattern of retreat presented in these verses which may be recognized by those who have obeyed the promptings of the Holy Spirit to set apart time with God in solitude. It involves areas of self-questioning under the Spirit's guidance, the awareness of one's own inability and helplessness, and then the process of being drawn into deeper and closer confrontation with God. Then Elijah hears an existential question, and there is no evasion: 'What are you doing here, Elijah?'

Of course, retrospectively, Elijah could have replied: 'Well *you* have brought me here, Lord – I am hardly responsible for where I am or how I feel.' But instead, confronted by the divine presence he opens his heart in confession and defeat, in brokenness and obedience. God does not immediately answer his questions, solve his problems or question his evaluation. Instead, he commands him to stand in the entrance of the cave on mount Horeb 'before the Lord'.

This suddenly becomes a very holy place. The confrontation turns out to be an unfolding of the divine Love. The unearthly phenomena of natural powers herald the silence of God. We stand with Elijah as the Lord passes by, and hear and feel the heralds of his divine presence:

> And behold, the LORD passed by, and a great and strong wind rent the mountains, and broke in pieces the rocks before the LORD, but the LORD was not in the wind; and after the wind an earthquake, but the LORD was not in the earthquake; and after the earthquake a fire, but the LORD was not in the fire; and after the fire a still small voice. . . . And when Elijah heard it, he wrapped his face in his mantle. . . .

We are used to the traditional still small voice, but the literal Hebrew rendering is 'a sound of gentle stillness' – a kind of ghostly calm that is so still it can be felt . . . be heard. Using the traditional words, the Quaker hymn writer catches the moment:

> Breathe through the heats of our desire
>   Thy coolness and Thy balm;
> Let sense be dumb – let flesh retire;
>   Speak through the earthquake, wind, and fire,
> O still small voice of calm.

References

1 Jer. 23:29.
2 Acts 9:1–19; 22:6–16; 26:12–18.
3 Acts 7:59f.
4 *English Praise*, No. 54.
5 See: Miguel de Unamuno, *The Tragic Sense of Life*, (Collins), pp. 182f.
6 *The New English Hymnal*, No. 350.

7 Romans 8:28.
8 I Tim. 6:15f.
9 Exod. 34:29–35.
10 1 Cor. 3:7–11.
11 I Cor. 3:18.
12 Matt.17:2; Mark 9:2.
13 Acts 7:56.
14 II Kings 2:11.
15 Matt. 17:10–13.
16 Col. 1:24–29; Jer. 31:33–34; Ezek. 36:26, 27.
17 See I Kings 17:8–24.
18 I Cor. 10:12.
19 Cf. James 4:7; and 2 Tim. 2:22.
20 Exod. 24:18; 34:28; Mark 1:13; Luke 4:2.
21 See the note on Exodus 19:16 in *The Interpreter's Bible*, Vol. I, p. 977. Cf. Judg. 5:4, 5; Isa. 2:12–22; Ps. 29.

B. New Testament Fruition

The roots of revelation in the New Testament are buried deep in Old Testament soil, and there is clear continuity in both mystical and prophetic experience. The role of the creative and life-giving Spirit of God becomes more prominent in the New Testament. Under the Old Covenant he is known to be the cosmic generative force in creation, and the mover and inspirer of the prophets. This continues to be true under the New Covenant, but he is also experienced corporately and individually as the indwelling Spirit of God, fulfilling the most sublime prophecies of the Old Testament.[1] John the Baptist, in the spirit and power of Elijah,[2] spans the old and new covenants. He was a man of the wilderness, spending his childhood in the desert places. He is therefore in continuity with the great prophetic tradition, and is the forerunner of the Messiah and Saviour of the New Testament. John's birth was surrounded by mystery, his preparation was in solitude, his ministry in the wilderness and his martyrdom in the desert fortress of Machaerus near the shores of the Dead Sea. This contributes to our theme of retreat, and indicates that such a theme includes the dark and basic facts of loneliness, aridity, self-questioning and death, as well as the prophetic joys of inspiration, proclamation, conversion and discipleship.

John's Preparation (Luke 1:5–25; 57–80)

In the prophetic tradition, John was a child of promise[3] given to Elizabeth and Zechariah in old age, as Isaac had been to Abraham and Sarah. Like Samuel, he was given to God, and the activity of the Holy Spirit bears witness to his prophetic vocation. After the extensive description of promise and fulfilment in his birth, Luke makes the important statement: 'And the child grew, and waxed strong in spirit, and was in the deserts till the day of his manifestation to Israel.'

John's vocation was not to follow his father into priesthood in the temple. His youth is shrouded in desert mystery which some have thought to have been spent with the monastic Essene community at Qumran near the Dead Sea.[4] Be that as it may, John's wilderness was Judea, the mountainous area to the east and south of Jerusalem, along the Jordan and the Dead Sea. John probably had some contact with the Essene monks, and the evidence makes it probable that his person and prophetic teaching were influenced by them. They ate locusts, did not partake of strong drink, and practised baptisms. They made a special study of the prophecy of Isaiah which the synoptic gospels quote in relation to John's ministry,[5] and in the *Rule of Qumran* we read the very words applied to the Essene monks which the gospel writers use of John the Baptist:

When these things shall come to pass in the Community of Israel, in accord with its destiny, let them depart from the city of men into the desert, to make a highway for the Lord as it is written: Prepare ye in the wilderness the way of the Lord. Make straight in the desert a highway for our God! The study of the Law, which God gave to Moses, is necessary if one is to act in accordance with what is revealed to each generation, and in accordance with what the prophets have revealed by God's Holy Spirit.[6]

The gospels are silent about any Essene connection, and in any case, John's wilderness training was basically in solitude and asceticism. He was neither a political revolutionary nor a rabbinical purist, but a prophet burdened with the divine Word and the divine Spirit.

John's Ministry (Matt. 3:1–17; Mark 1:1–11; Luke 3:1–22; John 1:6–8; 19–35)

John's preparation was born in wilderness prayer and contemplation, and his task was to be the forerunner, baptizer and proclaimer of the Lamb of God, the Messiah of Israel. Any vocation or ministry we may receive from God must be born in prayer and the interior desert of our hearts, for only such Spirit-inspired experience can prepare us for the work of ministry. There was a close link between the messianic preaching of John and the mystical vision of Jesus at his baptism. John the Evangelist makes this link, connecting the prophetic preparation of John the Baptist with the gospel themes of light, life and love.[7] His ministry was in utter yieldedness and was completely self-effacing. After declaring that Jesus, and not he, was Messiah, John the Baptist comments: 'He must increase, but I must decrease.' And so it was! It was a ministry conceived by the Holy Spirit, and only a rich interior and contemplative life, with its roots deep into wilderness soil, could bear such fruit. A negative form of retreat which evades truth and reality cannot sustain a vocation such as John's. He did not dwell in the wilderness for the sake of refreshment of spirit, but in order to be sanctified and transfigured by the Spirit of God into a vessel fit for the Master's use.

John's Martyrdom (Mark 6:21–29)

John the Baptist has always been held in high esteem in the Church, and especially by contemplative Orders and hermits who value the desert tradition. His birth *and* martyrdom are kept in the liturgical celebration, and this is not the case even with the apostles. Jesus himself, after striking commendatory words concerning John's prophetic stature, said: 'Truly, I say to you, among those born of women there has risen no one greater than John the Baptist. . . .'

He emerges from the mystery of his wilderness preparation, and after his brief but powerful ministry is confined to a prison cell and faced with death. He enters into the dark night of the senses and of the soul in which everything is taken from him, and he traverses an interior and arid desert that he has never before experienced. This passage is well known to the Desert Fathers' tradition and has a special relevance to the desert hermit in his cell. As I wrote those words, a pigeon flew out of the wide sky and crashed, but gently, against the window, and now sits blinking on the sill, observing me at work. In the midst of a consideration of John the Baptist's interior darkness I am reminded of the significance of the baptismal dove which appeared at Jesus' baptism to the eyes of John. And I am reminded of the powerful significance of the story of John languishing in his prison cell faced with the stark reality of imprisonment leading to death. The tremendous influence of this story on my own vocation and solitude is recounted in the chapter from which this book takes its title.[8]

The strength and courage given to John in the prison cell were the fruit of his years of wilderness solitude. He was not strengthened by his ministry – rather that very ministry and his present darkness are made meaningful by his interior life of prayer. It is only as we develop our inward contemplative lives that we shall be able to face, suffer and endure the joy and sorrow before us.

We do not know if we shall be called to a powerful and significant ministry, to fulfil an insignificant role of simple faithfulness in our daily lives of service, or whether we shall have to seal the testimony of Christ with our blood in martyrdom. But for any or all of these things we shall need to know the interior desert life that John knew, according to our own capacity – but desert life at *some* level. John's martyrdom prefigured to Jesus the consequences of his own ministry as the Suffering Servant of Isaiah, and the roots of it all are found in the preparation of John in the wilderness during the days of his youth and young manhood. The call of the desert is the preparation for the Gospel, and the call of the desert is the dynamic of ministry, and the preparation for a good death.

John the Baptist spent his formative years, from infancy

to young manhood, in a geographical and spiritual interior desert. Those thirty years or so prepared him for a brief period of amazing ministry and for a martyr's death in the dark solitude of the Dead Sea fortress. If such interior solitude was required for him for such a short ministry, we would do well to look at the quality of our own lives of prayer, and the consequnces in our ministry.

Mary, the Mother of Jesus (Luke 1:26–56; 2:22–52; John 19:25–27)

When we examine the pages of scripture in terms of the prophetic and apostolic vision and the solitude and retreat in which such vision is cradled and nurtured, we are soon brought to a consideration of Mary, the mother of Jesus. She relates the Old Covenant to the New Covenant; she is the womb of Israel and the image of the Church. Historically she was the mother of Jesus, and theologically the bearer of the Eternal Word.

Everything about her is gentle and yet strong. She is not called into a geographical wilderness for protracted periods of conflict, though carrying Jesus in her womb, she did go up into the Judean hill country to spend three months in quiet reflection with Elizabeth. But Mary's solitude was primarily one of the heart, for her interior life was rich and contemplative.

In the account of the Annunciation we have the beautiful narrative of the angel Gabriel's visit to Mary to announce the conception of Jesus in her virgin womb. To be pregnant with the Eternal Word is something we cannot begin to comprehend, but what a pattern it sets for the contemplative soul. Three times a day, when the Angelus bell rings in the monastery, we become quiet just where we are, and reflect upon the mystery of the Incarnation, and of Mary's courageous and obedient assent: 'Behold, I am the handmaid of the Lord; let it be to me according to your word.'

Gabriel told Mary that Elizabeth also had conceived a son and was six months pregnant, and some time later, Mary made her way up into the Judean hill country to reflect, pray and share with Elizabeth something of the wonder of the God who brings life out of nothing, and plants the divine seed within the contemplative heart and womb. The result of such a meeting was that the baby leaped in Elizabeth's womb to greet Mary with immense joy! And as Luke tells the story, the powerful words of the Magnificat are poured forth at this point.

Joy and Suffering

Shortly after the birth of Jesus, in the Lucan text, the story of the visit of the Bethlehem shepherds is recounted, with their description of the angelic vision and song. Mary listens with quiet wonder, and the text says that 'Mary kept all these things, pondering them in her heart.'

Mary is filled with the wonder of the divine initiative and of the contemplative joy that surrounded the nativity of Jesus. But she knew intuitively that wherever there was love and creativity there was inevitably the potential for sadness and suffering. Soon such a prophetic word was to be spoken to her, for when Joseph and Mary took the child Jesus to the temple to present him to the Lord, they were led to the old man Simeon. He had received a revelation from the Holy Spirit that he would not die until he had set eyes upon the Messiah. In the middle of his inspired words of blessing Mary felt her heart drawn out in love, and then suddenly chilled, as Simeon suddenly directed his words to her: 'Behold this child is set for the fall and rising of many in Israel, and for a sign that is spoken against . . . and a sword will pierce through your own soul also . . .'

The passing of the years only increased the love and longing in Mary's heart as she tended Jesus, watched and cared for him, holding him and yet allowing him the freedom of growth in wisdom and discernment. These are years of silence as far as scripture is concerned, covering approximately the same period when the boy and young man John the Baptist matured in the wilderness. But there is a significant moment recorded when Mary and Joseph took Jesus to Jerusalem when he was twelve years old. In the great company returning together after the feast, they supposed Jesus was with them. But after three days' searching they returned to Jerusalem and eventually found him debating and discussing with the doctors of the law in the temple. Mary took in the whole scene at once, voicing her perplexity, but receiving Jesus' answer interiorly: 'Why is it that you sought me? Did you not know that I must be in my Father's house?' Jesus then followed them obediently, and Luke records again: ' . . . and his mother kept all these things in her heart.'

Mary at the Cross

When one begins the ascent from the road up the track which leads to our monastery at Glasshampton, getting the first glimpse of the solitary, red brick building, the feeling of quietness and pilgrimage engendered becomes part of the journey. I feel it especially after having been away for a few days, for there is a solitary splendour about the way in which the monastery is situated high in the Worcestershire countryside. The monastery is dedicated to *St Mary at the Cross*, and the thing that struck me forcibly when I first approached it was the inscription below the clock tower: 'There stood at the Cross of Jesus, Mary his mother.'

In the chapel, which is the heart of the monastery, we have a large reproduction of the icon of *Our Lady of Vladimir*. The gentle tenderness and compassion of the face and hands of that icon indicate the interior life of Mary – a tenderness and compassion which include the wonder and grief of Bethlehem, Nazareth and Calvary. This is born of a whole life spent in a contemplative pondering within the heart. For when once the soul is given in glad surrender to God, then one's participation in the objective happenings and external circumstances of one's life become fuel for the contemplative life of prayer and intercession.

It is not easy to communicate to many who today want to jump on the 'contemplative band-wagon' that it is not a matter of learning a new (or ancient) technique; it is not acquiring a new skill, or the attainment of an intellectual or psychic manipulative faculty. These things may be offered by esoteric cults parading under the name of Christian or other labels, but they are not what the Christian contemplative life is about. Such a life and a way of prayer is a gospel way. It is a joyful, but also a difficult way. It has its spontaneity and ecstasy, but it also has its aridity and discipline. And there is no substitute for the thorny road and the dark night of the soul.

It is important that this be recognized, for it is too late

to expect to draw deep spiritual resources of strength and faith from a shallow and superficial life of prayer when sickness, bereavement or death confront one. Of course there is 'dying grace' for those who, like the one thief on the cross, cry out in penitence and faith, but life must not be lived out in neglect of spiritual values, in anticipation of such dying grace. As Bishop Ryle once said: 'One thief was saved that none might despair; but only one, that none might presume.'

Mary at the Cross is a picture of the contemplative soul plunged into the midst of desolation and grief, and yet sustained by the dying love of the Saviour who has himself plumbed the depths of desolation and dereliction. Only she could understand him, and only he could understand her. The contemplative sharing in love and grief is the moment of truth. Transfiguration begins its mighty work at the foot of the cross.

As a child I remember seeing a large Victorian print. It depicted the scene at the end of the day in the carpenter's shop at Nazareth. Joseph stood to the side and Jesus stood centrally behind the workbench, with sawdust and shavings around his feet. The boy Jesus stretches his arms as the westward sun causes his shadow to fall on the wall behind. Along that central wall was a large rack with hammers, mallets and nails in their places, and the outstretched arms of Jesus are silhouetted there. Mary enters the shop just at that moment, and the look upon her face gives the title to the picture: *The Shadow of the Cross*.

This is what spiritual retreat is all about. It is the inward journey of the contemplative soul in union with the Lord. It is the pondering of the heart, the experience and expression of the profound joy and wonder, the grief and suffering of birth and life and death and resurrection – St Mary at the Cross.

> Who, on Christ's dear mother gazing,
> Pierced by anguish so amazing,
>   Born of woman, would not weep?
> Who, on Christ's dear mother thinking,
> Such a cup of sorrow drinking,
>   Would not share her sorrows deep?

Jesus, may her deep devotion
Stir in me the same emotion
    Fount of love, Redeemer kind,
That my heart, fresh ardour gaining,
And a purer love attaining,
    May with Thee acceptance find.

Attrib. Jacapone da Todi

The Hidden Life of Jesus

It is in the life of Jesus, *par excellence*, that we become aware of the hidden dimension of the life of contemplative prayer. There are constant references to lonely places, spending all night in prayer, hours of sacred tryst with the Father on the mountain. But quite apart from all those periods of physical withdrawal and retreat, there is the awareness of the fact that Jesus carried with him an interior stillness, and a dimension of contemplation in which he was continually living, walking, moving in the Holy Spirit. The Spirit was given to him without measure, and he did and said those things which continually manifested and glorified the Father. And all this because he lived and matured over the years of young manhood in the school of obedience and prayer.

There is a tendency, in these 'charismatic' days, to move from charism to witness prematurely and at a superficial level – from a first, or new experience of God, into a proclamation situation, without profound contemplative reflection. In the prophetic tradition, as we have seen, following upon the revelation there was a time of waiting and reflection in order that the vision and message might root itself deeply within the soul. New converts may have zeal but they do not always have wisdom and maturity. Between the powerful accounts of Jesus' baptism in the synoptic gospels and his preaching with great power in Galilee there is the period of retreat and conflict in the wildneress. It is unavoidable!

Jesus in the Wilderness (Matt. 4:1–11; Mark 1:12, 13; Luke 4:1–13)

Jesus did not move immediately from his baptism and anointing with the Spirit into the arena of proclamation and service. First of all there were retreat, wilderness, conflict, temptation and victory. This was accompanied by fasting and prayer over a period of weeks within the context of the spiritual world of darkness and light, with satanic and angelic intervention. Only then, after the baptism of power and trial was Jesus prepared and equipped to proclaim and demonstrate the Kingdom of God.

Mark's brief reference to the temptation is powerful, occurring immediately after his account of Jesus' baptism: 'The Spirit immediately drove him out into the wilderness. And he was in the wilderness forty days, tempted by Satan; and he was with the wild beasts; and the angels ministered to him.'

The gospel writers use two different words to indicate Jesus' entry into the wilderness. Matthew and Luke state that he was 'led' by the Holy Spirit, (*anagō*), whereas Mark maintains that he was 'driven' (*ekballō*). This is an instance of one of the forceful expressions of Mark, quite in keeping with the Old Testament understanding of the dynamic and objective power of the Spirit which came upon, moved and wrestled with men. Certainly we may translate the account of the temptation into spiritual and psychological terms when we apply the situation to our own lives, but we must not forget the objectivity of the account in the gospels and the fact that our dealings with God, and with dark powers, cannot be wholly contained within psychological categories.

But there may also be times when we feel ourselves driven into a wilderness, into which the Spirit leads or drives us, according to his will. And we shall then 'beat a retreat' from the multiplicity of worldly demands to give attention to the interior life of glory or conflict.

The 'forty days' of the wilderness again indicate that Jesus was in the prophetic tradition, recalling Moses upon the mountain of glory, Elijah on Horeb, and Israel's forty years of wandering in the desert.[9] Jesus was not only the fulfilment of the prophetic vocation, but he was the last Adam, the representative Man, recapitulating in his human life the corporate nature of human experience. He was in the wilderness for us just as surely as he was crucified for us. And that is why we need to enter with him into our wilderness and Calvary experience, if we are truly to be Christians:

> For us He was baptized, and bore
> His holy fast, and hungered sore;
> For us temptations sharp He knew;
> For us the tempter overthrew.[10]

There is an interesting reference in the *Testament of Naphtali* 8:4, to the wilderness experience: 'And the devil will flee away from you, and the wild beasts will fear you, and angels will come unto you'. But the reference to wild beasts in Mark may well indicate not that they were fearful, but that as in some Franciscan story, they proclaim a return to paradise, the Edenic state in which 'the second Adam to the fight and to the rescue came'.

Conflict with Dark Powers

But now we come to the main thrust of these wilderness accounts. The gospel writers are not here portraying Jesus in the context of a wilderness retreat of tranquillity and peace. There *are* such times for the child of God, and part of this book is taken up with commending such times. But here the retreat becomes conflict, and Jesus is thrust not into an attitude of defence but of attack. He is led and driven into the wilderness in the fulness of the Holy Spirit, and there engages in spiritual warfare, combat, conflict, wrestling, with the great Adversary. 'For we are not contending against flesh and blood, but against the principalities, against the powers, against the world rulers of this present darkness, against the spiritual hosts of wickedness in the heavenly places.'[11]

There is a sense, of course, in which we are always engaged in spiritual warfare, for whenever we give ourselves to light and love and truth, we oppose the dominions of darkness, hatred and deceit. But there are times when the athlete of God is called not only into competition, but into conflict in a concentrated manner. The deeper life of prayer is primarily for the sake of the divine love and for the sanctification of the whole world. But there is an inevitable confrontation with powers of darkness in this dimension of prayer. And the prerequisites for such a life are a boundless humility and a fulness of the Holy Spirit. Those who 'dabble' in the areas of the spiritual without such preparedness are in grave moral and spiritual danger. And this applies to the powers of light as well as of darkness. The holiness of God can smite a man as well as the occult powers of darkness.

Four Levels of Retreat

It is sufficient for us at present to see that our Lord knew times of retreat upon the mountain, in solitary places, and in the wilderness, for at least four reasons. First of all there was that primary and basic need in him to dwell within the bosom of the Father continually. Not only to gaze upon the divine glory and to rest in the divine love, but to participate continually in the divine trinitarian life. We cannot understand the pain or the splendour of the incarnate life of Jesus, but we glimpse such unearthly yearnings in passages such as the high priestly prayer of St John's Gospel:

> I glorified thee on earth, having accomplished the work which thou gavest me to do; and now, Father, glorify thou me in thy own presence with the glory which I had with thee before the world was made.[12]

Following upon such a primary and basic necessity for our Lord to maintain the continual flow of communion with the Father by the indwelling Spirit, there was secondly the need for physical, mental and spiritual refreshment – a kind of recharging of the batteries. There were times when physical and spiritual power went out of him in his compassion for the sick and needy. As Mark comments concerning one of the healing miracles: 'Jesus, perceiving in himself that power (*dunamis*) had gone forth from him, immediately turned about in the crowd, and said, "Who touched me?" and the woman who had suffered from an internal haemorrhage for twelve years owned up that she had 'felt in her body that she was healed of her disease.' We read that as many as touched him on certain occasions were made whole, and that as a result of his ministry, unclean spirits fell down before him in submission. The result of such a psychosmatic and spiritual ministry was that he needed constantly to be renewed and refreshed, so that he withdrew into solitude for himself, and with his disciples when they were involved in the apostolic ministry of preaching, teaching and healing.

Thirdly there was the matter of guidance and direction. Before our Lord chose and called his apostles there was a prolonged period of waiting upon the Father – retreat before an important decision. Luke records it succinctly:

In these days he went out into the hills to pray; and all night he continued in prayer to God. And when it was day, he called his disciples, and chose from them twelve, whom he named apostles.[13]

Prayer in the solitude of the hills at night enabled Jesus to choose an apostolic Peter who would be transformed by his conversion into the leader of the apostles. But it also enabled him to choose Judas who was of the stuff of a betrayer and who would eventually hand Jesus over to the authorities to be crucified. Both were caught up into the wider purposes of God, and woven into the pattern of redemption.

These three levels of prayer and retreat include communion, contemplation, adoration and direction. There is a fourth dimension of retreat which has to do with conflict. Because our Lord Jesus was in constant communion with the Father, and anointed with the power of the Holy Spirit, he was able to enter into spiritual combat with, and overthrow, the powers of darkness. This certainly took place over a prolonged period in the wilderness of the temptation stories, but there were other areas of conflict, right up to and including the crucifixion. Jesus saw the overthrow of Satan in prophetic insight and demonstrated such in his miracles of healing and exorcism: 'I saw Satan fall like lightning from heaven.' And as Paul extols Christ as the *Christus Victor*, he writes of his atoning work upon the cross: 'He disarmed the principalities and powers, and made a public example of them, triumphing over them.'[14]

I am not suggesting that everyone who reads these pages will become engaged in direct spiritual confrontation with dark powers, or will be exposed at the levels we have spoken of. But it is necessary to know about them, and of the direction that the life of prayer may carry a believer who takes God seriously and who responds to that deep, inward call to contemplative prayer.

There is much superficial and glossy charismatic literature which errs greatly on two levels. On the one hand it has a matey and undemanding attitude in terms of an understanding of the being and character or God, resulting in badly based theological and psychological teaching. On the other hand there is a glut of writing about the occult, exorcism, spiritual discernment and demon possession which sometimes betrays a misreading of psychological and psychosomatic illness, and sometimes underestimates the 'depths of Satan' and exposes the practitioner and his audience to spiritual harm.

We have just referred to Jesus' calling of the apostolic band after a period of prayer in the hills. Mark gives a concise listing of the reasons for the calling of the apostles:

> to be with him,
> to preach,
> to cast out demons[15]

Failure in the latter two tasks in the disciples' early ministry could always be traced to failure in the first. To be with Jesus, to gaze upon him, to dwell within him – as he dwelt within the Father. I have been many years on the way of Jesus, and still find myself returning to the place of silence and adoration where I dwell within the bosom of the Father. And often in my success or failure in the apostolic task I find myself singing:

> Jesus! I am resting, resting
>   In the joy of what Thou art;
> I am finding out the greatness
>   Of Thy loving heart.
> Thou hast bid me gaze upon Thee,
>   And Thy beauty fills my soul,
> For, by Thy transforming power,
>   Thou hast made me whole.

Jesus on the Mount of Transfiguration (Matt. 17:1–9; Mark 9:2–8; Luke 9:28–36)

We turn from the picture of Jesus in the wilderness to Jesus on the holy mountain. From temptation to Transfiguration. There are so many moments of illumination in this whole radiant passage that one can envisage many years of contemplative meditation being spent in its transfiguring light. Jesus' glory is above the brightness of the sun and we can capture only some of the rays that shine into our hearts. There was an old Welsh pulpit which had written within it, for the preacher's eyes only: 'Sir, we would see Jesus'. Jesus only is the centre of this story of the Transfiguration, for gazing upon his loveliness all else fades into insignificance. One of my Sunday School teachers once told me that he had heard an apprentice-boy going about his work whistling and singing:

> Turn your eyes upon Jesus,
> Look full in his wonderful face;
> And the things of earth will grow strangely dim
> In the light of his glory and grace.

And as he told me, his own face shone with the radiance of Jesus' love. His glory outshines the sun and his presence causes the thundering of Moses' law and the power of Elijah's prophecy to fade away. When Jesus appears in his glory, clothed within and without in the uncreated energies of God, and anointed with the sevenfold power of the Holy Spirit, then all that can be glimpsed, heard or grasped in those moments is the voice from the eternal world: 'This is my beloved Son, with whom I am well pleased; listen to him.' The petrine group in the early church preserves the apostolic testimony from the mouth of Peter:

> We did not follow cleverly devised myths when we made known to you the power and coming of our Lord Jesus Christ, but we were eye-witnesses of his majesty. For when he received honour and glory from God the Father and the voice was borne to him by the Majestic Glory, 'This is my beloved Son, with whom I am well pleased,'

we heard this voice borne from heaven, for we were with him on the holy mountain.[16]

The word which Luke uses for 'eyewitness' means primarily one who sees with his own eyes. In the above quotation the word used is one which is employed in the Greek Eleusinian mysteries for the initiate who had achieved the highest level of insight. Both meanings are operative here, for the apostles were not only reporting and proclaiming objective facts, but were also witnessing to the interior truth and significance of the Transfiguration.

I have written elsewhere of the overflowing and transfiguring power of Christ in the experience, bodily and spiritually, of those who spend time with him on the holy mountain of contemplation. But here I want to call attention to an even more basic and important matter. It is that we do not believe that adoration and worship end in Jesus. That would be 'Jesusolatry'. Jesus is the Way – the Way to the Father. He is the one Mediator between God and men. He is the reconciling Saviour who gathers up our penitence and faith, our love, adoration and worship, and carries us with it all into the mystery, into the glory and splendour of the Father. On the mount of Transfiguration the disciples gazed upon the unutterable glory of the Holy Trinity. This is expounded in the three gospel accounts, and is set within the trinitarian theology of the passage from the second epistle of Peter.

From twelve years of age I was brought up in a warm evangelical atmosphere, in which glory and worship were ascribed to Jesus Christ as Lord. There was some quite clear trinitarian teaching, but it was not always clear that worship was offered to the Father in the name of the Son and by the power of the Holy Spirit. I remember being quite perplexed and confused as I heard the extempore prayers in the weekly devotional service. 'Father' and 'Jesus' were frequently interchanged in one prayer, and apart from a few hymns, prayers were rarely addressed to the Holy Spirit. I am grateful for all the blessings of such an evangelical background, but later objective liturgical worship grounded in scripture did make God the Father the fountain, source and goal of all worship and adoration.

49

This has also been the experience of my life of prayer. The saving and healing power of the Lord Jesus, and the indwelling of the Holy Spirit have brought me into an ever more profound understanding of the incomprehensible mystery of the Father. The more I learn theologically, and the more I experience spiritually in the life of prayer, so the more I realize that I have to learn, know and experience. I feel this personally as a child of God, and appreciate it corporately with my brothers and sisters in the Body of Christ. There is a whole cosmic redemptive movement in which the whole creation is moving towards the fulness of redemption in Christ.

And all this is reflected in the story of the Transfiguration. Already the divine uncreated energies of God are at work in the world. The cosmos reflects the transfiguring glory of God in the face and garments of Jesus. The glory overflows to the disciples, includes the Old Testament saints Moses and Elijah, and all are caught up in the prophetic, redemptive process which moves towards the goal of unity in the Holy Trinity.

The Feast of the Transfiguration on the 6th August is a most important feast in the Orthodox Churches of the East, and much is made of the symbol of light in Eastern spirituality. This feast has become increasingly celebrated in the Western Church, and it is also a harrowing experience, for it now commemorates the dropping of the first atomic bomb on Hiroshima on 6th August 1945. This in itself is sufficient to cause us to set the day aside to consider the glory of God and the misery of mankind, and in our lives of prayer to bridge the great gulf between.

I lived with the Community of the Transfiguration, near Edinburgh, before entering the Society of St Francis. It is a small and simple hut community, living a very basic gospel life. When the community began in the 1960s the brothers were given use of the famous Roslin Chapel. When they descended into the otherwise dark crypt about six feet below ground level they were faced with a beautiful stained glass window of the Transfiguration with words from Psalm 36: *'In lumine tuo videbimus lumen'* – 'In your light we see light.' They took that as a sign that it was the right place for them – and so it proved to be.

The Transfiguration is a dramatic invitation to prayer and identification with the glory and compassion of God in Jesus for us today, for it was from the holy mount that Jesus descended with his disciples into the plain of human helplessness and need. From the holy mount he brought to the impotent disciples below his enabling power, and to the sick and sorrowful the healing and light of the Gospel. This serves then as a pattern for retreat and prayer, equipping us for loving service in the world.

Jesus in the Garden of Gethsemane (Matt. 26:36–46; Mark 14:32–42; Luke 22:40–46)

I write these words on the Wednesday of Holy Week. Tomorrow, Maundy Thursday, at our small monastery here in Worcester, we shall be celebrating the Mass of the Lord's Supper, and enacting the washing of feet ceremony when the brothers and guests will have their feet washed by the priest kneeling before them as Jesus commanded.[17] Then the consecrated bread and wine will be carried to the altar of repose from which we shall receive communion on Good Friday. The last thing we shall do before setting up the night watch at the altar of repose will be to strip the altar and chapel bare, in memory of the stripping and forsaking of Jesus in the Garden of Gethsemane and Calvary while the priest and brothers say Psalm 22, the psalm of crucifixion. I always find this a lonely and dark experience, for it brings forcibly to mind the way in which our Lord was stripped, forsaken and made desolate in the last hours of his earthly life.

I well remember the intense religious experience of the Garden of Gethsemane when I lived in the wooden hut during my six months of solitude in Dorset in 1982. I was called out of the hut at 4.00 a.m., and as I stood prayerfully near a clump of bushes and trees I felt I was in the company of Peter, James and John, watching the Lord Jesus, just a stone's throw away, on his face upon the ground, pleading with his Father, and sweating, as it were, great drops of blood. That was a heavy experience for me, for I felt my own helplessness, together with that of the three disciples, and felt the pain of those words: 'So, could you not watch with me one hour? Watch and pray that you may not enter into temptation; the spirit indeed is willing, but the flesh is weak.'[16]

The three disciples who had companied with Jesus upon the mount of Transfiguration were also called into the mystery of Gethsemane. Where did these accounts come from except from them, especially as they portray the spiritual and emotional suffering in the aptly named Garden of Gethsemane (oil-press)? Judas had already gone down the road to betray Jesus; eight of the disciples had been left somewhere near the entrance to the garden, and the three were apprehensively waiting in the shadows. As someone has written: 'He himself went in loneliness a little farther – the distance of a whole eternity.' And while he retreated into an agony of prayer – they slept!

During this Holy Week we have been reading over and over again the story of the Passion, and on Palm Sunday, and again on Good Friday, the story will be read and chanted by three brothers in parts. As a background to the gospel story we are reading, at morning and evening prayer, the Lamentations and the Prophecy of Jeremiah. The whole solitary sorrow of this week takes us deeper into the contemplation of the Lamb of God, the Man of Sorrows, the wounded, dying Saviour of the World, in all his loneliness and pain. The gospel writers are very explicit in the way they speak of the interior grief and emotional pain of Jesus:

> . . . and he began to be sorrowful and troubled. Then he said to them, 'My soul is very sorrowful, even to death; remain here and watch with me. . . .'

These are Matthew's words. And Mark uses an even stronger word for 'sorrowful' which could be rendered 'distressed' or even 'terrified'. Translators use terms like 'appalled and agitated', and 'distress and dread'. They are saying that Jesus was facing terrors unknown before, not merely the physical aspects of torture and death, which he shared with many before and after him, but all that it meant to be on the road to Calvary, as the Lamb of God who bears the sin of the world. All the prophesied sorrow and burden of the Suffering Servant of Isaiah's prophecy was before him, and the shadow of the Cross had become an awful reality:

> See him prostrate in the Garden,
> On the ground your Maker lies!
> On the awful Tree behold him
> Hear him cry before he dies:
>   'It is finished!'
> Sinner, will not this suffice?

Gethsemane and Calvary are all of a piece in our Saviour's work of redemption, and as we contemplate Gethsemane, Calvary and the darkness of the tomb, we are drawn into participation, into the fellowship of his sufferings. When I was Anglican Chaplain to the University of Glasgow and on the staff of St Mary's Cathedral, some of the students would spend the whole night in watching and prayer on Maundy Thursday. There was coffee available in the vestry, and wrapped in cloaks and overcoats in the candlelit church we watched and prayed alone and together in waking and sleeping through the night. It is difficult to explain, but it was both a beautiful and a sorrowful experience. There was a kind of fellowship of love and suffering, a deep desire to enter more deeply into our Lord's grief and passion, and at the same time an almost palpable love for him in and through one another. In the morning we were loth to leave the Cathedral and to walk through the Good Friday morning down the Great Western Road in Glasgow – into a city and a world full of the sorrow and pain for which Jesus died.

This is the quality of fellowship and worship, the sharing of suffering and compassion that our Lord desires to beget in us in our life of prayer. This is why he calls us apart, into retreat, into the wilderness, up into the mountain, into the garden, to draw near to him, to gaze upon him, to dwell within him.

Every Holy Week it is the same, and always that desire to be identified more closely with Jesus in his passion and death is strengthened, and, I pray, made more real. I look back over the last decade or so, and see into St Mary's, the small group praying before the candle-lit altar of repose, the sprinkling of young and old around the rest of the church, and the few sleeping across and under some of the pews for an hour, to renew their watch again . . . all longing for the light and joy of Easter. And I pray for them all again – where they are now – loving and serving God in his world.

Jesus . . . in the days of his flesh

We have followed our Lord in three aspects of his life of prayer and solitude, in his Temptation, Transfiguration, and in the Garden of Gethsemane. All three demanded retreat and aloneness, although on two of the occasions his three disciples were not far away, though asleep. The Epistle to the Hebrews, in retrospect, looks toward Gethsemane and joyfully affirms the same Jesus as our Great High Priest, living in the power of an endless life, our Forerunner and Mediator, in the glory of the Father:

> In the days of his flesh, Jesus offered up prayers and supplications, with loud cries and tears, to him who was able to save him from death, and he was heard for his godly fear. Although he was a Son, he learned obedience through what he suffered; and being made perfect he became the source of eternal salvation to all who obey him, being designated by God a high priest after the order of Melchizedek.[19]

To accompany Jesus through Gethsemane to Calvary is only half the truth. The Easter glory is glimpsed through the darkness of Holy Week, but the Sun of Righteousness rises in all his glory on Easter Morning. The ceremonies of Holy Week culminate in the midnight or dawn Eucharist of Easter, with a loud and triumphant shout: CHRIST IS RISEN! In many churches, it is the custom at midnight, or just before dawn on Easter Day, to gather around a prepared brazier with a flint and the paschal candle to represent the new light struck in the tomb, which blazed forth and shone throughout the world.

I have always found this a tremendous experience, especially gathering in the darkness with a crowd of subdued but expectant people in the cold of the pre-Easter rising. When I spent my second period of six months' solitude on the edge of the Lleyn Peninsula, facing the Island of Bardsey, up to the Spring of 1984, I prepared a large bonfire on the desolate and deserted part of Anelog overlooking the sea. Just before midnight there was a stiff breeze blowing on a clear night with high sky above, and tiny lights twinkling in the village of Aberdaron two miles or so below. I had my paschal candle guarded from the breeze, and the glorious moment came when I struck my new fire and spread the flame to the bonfire.

In no time the paper and kindling were ablaze and I cried out:

> The Light of Christ
> *Thanks be to God!*
> Christ is risen
> *He is risen indeed!*

And then I broke into song as the bonfire blazed:

> Low in the grave he lay,
> Jesus, my Saviour,
> Waiting the coming day,
> Jesus, my Lord.
> *Up from the grave He arose,*
> *With a mighty triumph o'er His foes;*
> *He arose a victor from the dark domain,*
> *And He lives for ever with His saints to reign!*
> *He arose! He arose!*
> *Alleluia! Christ arose!*

One of the lovely things about that experience was that it was only a score or so miles from the Irish coast where Saint Patrick defied the pagan high-king Laoghaire on Easter eve, and kindled the paschal fire on the hill of Slane in the fifth century. Then too the Easter fire burned in the ancient Celtic Church and I felt the joy of continuing such glorious celebration fifteen centuries later on the Welsh coast. And I was not alone for the trail of such fires burned down the intervening centuries. I stayed in the warmth and light of that fire for a long time, and then processed into the little stone cottage with the pastoral candle, singing, to celebrate the Eucharist of Easter.[20]

Thus, following the pattern of the life of Jesus, especially in the Temptation, Transfiguration, suffering and Resurrection, it is evident how important retreat and solitude were to him. It was a life of gospel alternation – taking his disciples into desert places for refreshment and prayer, leading Peter, James and John into contemplation in joy and sorrow, and spending days and nights alone in the wilderness, upon the mountain, in communion with the Father, and yearning for the restoration of his pre-incarnate glory.[21]

This is the pattern of the life of every Christian. The development of such a life of retreat and prayer on this biblical principle will show great differences in the amount of time given to it, and at different periods in one's life, more or less time will be given. But there should emerge a pattern of prayer that increases in longing and in depth, sending down roots into scripture and solitude.

John on the Island of Patmos (Rev. 1:9, 10)

I John, your brother, who share with you in Jesus the tribulation and the kingdom and the patient endurance, was on the island called Patmos on account of the word of God and the testimony of Jesus. I was in the Spirit on the Lord's day, and I heard behind me a loud voice like a trumpet. . . .

These powerful words set the scene for the revelation which John receives in his island retreat of Patmos. The early tradition consistently says that he was banished in exile to Patmos in the reign of the persecuting Emperor Domitian. After Domitian's death and the repeal of some of the persecuting acts by the senate, he returned to Patmos and completed his writing of the Apocalypse. There was early dispute as to whether the book should have a place in the canon of scripture. This was true in the churches of Syria, Cappadocia and even of Palestine up to the fifth century. In Reformation times both Luther and Zwingli were hostile to it, and it is the one New Testament book which Calvin omitted from his exegetical works.

On the other hand Philip Carrington, writing perhaps in ignorance of the critical standpoint, but feeling the immediacy of the impact of its message says:

> In the case of the Revelation we are dealing with an artist greater than Stevenson or Coleridge or Bach. St John has a better sense of the right word than Stevenson; he has a greater command of unearthly, supernatural loveliness than Coleridge; he has a richer sense of melody and rhythm and composition than Bach. . . . It is the only masterpiece of pure art in the New Testament. . . . Its fulness and richness and harmonious variety place it far above Greek tragedy.

Apocalyptic Vision and Retreat

The controversy surrounding this book often reflects the age in which it is considered. Our references to John on Patmos substantiate our argument that prophetic vision is imparted in solitude and retreat. In this sense, John the Theologian is in direct line with the Old Testament prophets and patriarchs. But there is the added note of *apocalyptic*, and this kind of visionary writing is not acceptable in times of tranquillity and peace. The paradox here is that the revelation of apocalyptic vision with all its thunder, terror and bloodshed is conceived during a time of bloody persecution under Nero and Domitian, around 94 AD, on a barren, rocky little island off the coast of Asia Minor, in a vision of contemplative dimensions. Such is the importance of the book that Vernon Sproxton says that apart from the gospels and the Epistle to the Romans, John's visions on Patmos have had greater influence on religious aspiration and political ideology than any other part of the New Testament. It has both coloured Christians' dreams about what heaven is like, and has given a certain authority to those who would assume the 'Rule of the Saints' on earth.

Apocalyptic arises from persecution and an awareness of imminent cosmic disaster and was very popular in certain Jewish circles in the two centuries before Christ. Prophets like Ezekiel and Zechariah prepared the way, and the form was developed by Daniel's time, with many apocryphal writings at the beginning of the Christian era. The Book of the Revelation (*not* Revelations!) is the only apocalyptic document in the New Testament. It was relevant to the persecuting era at the end of the first century, and its relevance becomes operative again in these days when secular and religious prophets of doom are warning the world of possible cosmic nuclear catastrophe. R. H. Charles, in his commentary, *Revelation*, says that according to the Apocalypse, all faithful Christians are to expect martyrdom.

The very word *apocalypse*, rendered *revelation*, means an unveiling. It is the disclosure of doctrinal, prophetic and contemplative truth, and thrusts us into the vistas of eternity. There are great differences between the prophetic words of the early Old Testament prophets and the later prophets who incorporate apocalyptic vision of catastrophe and imminent destruction, linking them with the apocalyptic visionaries of inter-testamental times, up to the time of Christ. It is not my purpose to deal with this area, though it is a compulsive study, expounded in any reliable commentary on the Apocalypse.[22]

What is important for us is the fact that John the Theologian was a man of great prophetic, apocalyptic and contemplative vision, that he was exiled to a place of retreat 40 miles off the coast of Asia Minor, and that he was caught up into a series of contemplative and apocalyptic visions in which an unveiling was vouchsafed to him in the context of ecstasy, adoration and revelation. The geographical location afforded the wide vistas of earth, sea and sky, and natural phenomena contribute integrally to his symbolic communication of supernatural truth.

Apocalyptic and Contemplation
I affirmed earlier not only the compatibility, but the essential unity of prophetic and mystical vision in the Old Testament prophets. Prophetic religion is grounded and rooted in mystical vision. In this document, the mystical and contemplative vision is integral to the apocalyptic and prophetic word. It is the discernment and vision of a man of God in solitude which allows him to be caught up into

the divine world, primarily to behold the glory of the great God whose kingdom and sovereignty are eternal, and secondarily to teach and warn of the things which will shortly come to pass in terror and catastrophe upon the earth.

Contemporary Hermit Life

There has always been the element of conflict and confrontation in the classic hermit life, not only in terms of the hermit's own psychological darkness, but also with regard to dark cosmic powers. To a lesser degree this becomes operative in the life of any person who enters into the solitude of retreat with God. At no time did John the Theologian lose sight of the Body of Christ in his visions and writings. The pastoral and doctrinal needs of the seven churches of Asia Minor were immediately before him, and the awareness of the whole body of the communion of saints surrounded him and irradiated his vision. He was enveloped in a glory of revelation in which the twenty-four elders surrounding the throne were symbolic of the twelve patriarchs of the Old Testament and the twelve apostles of the New Testament. And these were only part of the adoring multitudes of angelic and other orders of being, prostrate in adoring wonder before the manifestation of the glory of the mysterious Godhead. This is powerful symbolic language:

Then I looked, and I heard around the throne and the living creatures and the elders the voice of many angels, numbering myriads of myriads and thousands of thousands, saying with a loud voice, 'Worthy is the Lamb who was slain, to receive power and wealth and wisdom and might and honour and glory and blessing!' And I heard every creature in heaven and on earth and under the earth and in the sea, and all therein, saying, 'To him who sits upon the throne and to the Lamb be blessing and honour and glory and might for ever and ever! And the four living creatures said, 'Amen!' And the elders fell down and worshipped.[23]

The hermit in his cell, in forest, mountain, desert or

island, is dynamically aware both of his own solitude and of the cosmic communion with earth and heaven. It is an awareness of light and darkness, and is both pagan and Christian. The pagan dimension has to do with the darkness of the old Adamic nature within himself, with the particular associations of the location of his desert, and with the dark powers which threaten the man of love and prayer. An important book of papers on the hermit life came out of the Symposium held at St Davids, Wales, in 1975, under the title *Solitude and Communion*, in which A. M. Allchin writes:

The life is one which demands considerable maturity, human and psychological, as well as ascetic and spiritual. It is not a way to be undertaken unadvisedly, lightly, or wantonly, and it will not ordinarily be undertaken without some considerable experience of a regular life of prayer and obedience lived in community.

Contemporary hermit life often has this element of the present darkness of this world within its theological vision and perspective. It is not that the hermit is led or driven into the wilderness primarily to enter into confrontation with dark powers, but rather that exposure to the divine mystery of Love is the primary thing, and the conflict with evil is a part of that revelatory and sanctifying pattern. Also, it is not that the contemporary hermit feels himself to be one with the great tradition in which confrontation with dark powers is an integral part, (though that is true), but that there is a particular contemporary darkness which threatens the fabric of the whole created order, at least in terms of our own world.

John the Theologian is aware of all this for his own time and age. His mystical and prophetic concerns are also pastoral concerns, and his vision of the divine glory includes the demonic invasion of dark powers. Central to his vision is the eternal mystery of God symbolized by the Throne, the Lamb and the Sevenfold Spirit – a trinitarian vision. But from the throne of incomprehensible mystery sounds the vision and voice of revelation:

I was in the Spirit on the Lord's day, and I heard behind me a loud voice like a trumpet saying, 'Write what you see in a book and send it to the seven churches, to Ephesus and to Smyrna and to Pergamum and to Thyatira and to Sardis and to Philadelphia and to Laodicea. . . '

The Call to Prophetic Contemplation

The power and apostolic nature of the Apocalypse may seem to be a far cry from our own inadequate understanding of the word and vision of God in our contempoary situation. But we are encouraged not to despise the day of small things. It does seem that God is not only reviving the vocation of the hermit and solitary life for certain people today, but also calling all members of Christ into a more contemplative and prophetic consideration of what it means to belong to the reconciling Body of Christ.

The Apocalypse itself is the result of John's obedience to the heavenly vision. The Spirit thrust him into the island retreat as Jesus was thrust into the wilderness for his confrontation with darkness. The result for both was revelation, confrontation and affirmation of the divine word which was communicated in scripture and in the ongoing life of the Church. Certainly Jesus stood before God in solidarity with the whole human race, and it was for us that he underwent his temptation and for us that he suffered his passion. John, on the island of Patmos, was also aware that he represented the Church to God, as he represented God to the Church. It is within this context of one belonging to all, and all represented in the one, that we can more fully understand the vocation to solitude for whatever length of time. This means that when a man hears the inward call to prayer and solitude, be it for a day, a month, a year, or for some unspecified period, he hears it for every member of the Body of Christ, and in these days of dis-integration and schism, this word of representative solidarity and unity is all the more needful.[24]

The Biblical Roots of Retreat into God

This chapter and the last have traversed the canon of scripture with seven league boots, but the aim is simple and clear: to affirm that wherever God has called men into a deeper union with himself, and has vouchsafed a vision of revelation and communication to his world, there has always been a period of solitude in some form of desert. This has served to be the locus of vision/revelation, and as a place of contemplative consideration and refreshment. It is usually followed by the communication of the revelation, together with a prophetic call to holiness, love and social righteousness.

From Adam to Malachi in the Old Testament, and from John the Baptist to John the Theologian in the New Testament the sotry is the same. There is, of course, much more to be said about the preparation, the content and the communication of the vision, but the element of retreat is indispensable, and its roots run deep into the soul of scripture.

References
1 Jer. 31:31–34; Ezek. 36:25–28.
2 Luke 1:17.
3 Mal. 3:1; 4:5–6.
4 See Jean Steinmann, 'Was John the Baptist an Essene?' *St John the Baptist*, (London: Longman), pp. 58ff.
5 Luke 3:4–6; Matt. 3:3; Mark 1:2–4.
6 Steinmann, ibid., p. 59.
7 Note the place of John the Baptist in *St John's Gospel*, Prologue.
8 See Matt. 11:1–6; Luke 7:19–23, and chapter thirteen, 'Deeper into God'.
9 Exod. 34:28; Josh. 5:6; 1 Kings 19:8.
10 *English Hymnal* No. 459.
11 Ephes. 6:12.
12 John 17:4, 5.
13 Luke 6:12, 13.
14 Col. 2:15.
15 Mark 3:14, 15.
16 2 Pet. 1:16–18; read on to verse 24.
17 John 13:1–9.
18 Matt 26:40, 41.
19 Heb. 5:7–10.

20 Living in a long period of solitude I had permission to celebrate the Eucharist.
21 John 17:13, 24.
22 a) Background and devotional use:
William Barclay, *The Revelation of John*, Vols. I and II (Edinburgh: St Andrew Press); Vernon Sproxton, *Good News in Revelation*; (Glasgow: Collins Fontana) *The Jerusalem Bible* (Study Edition), Introduction to the Revelation (London: Darton, Longman and Todd).
b) More serious study:
The Revelation to John in *The Interpreter's Bible*, Vol. XII (Nashville: Abingdon Press); H. B. Swete, *The Apocalypse of St John* (London: Macmillan); R. H. Charles, *Revelation*, ICC commentary (Edinburgh: T & T Clark).
23 Rev. 5:11–14.
24 This matter of the identification of the whole people with one man is well expounded in the thought of St Peter Damian to fellow-hermits, in the St Davids Symposium papers, *Solitude and Communion*, ed. A. M. Allchin (Oxford: Fairacre Publications), pp. 6ff.

3: The Desert Fathers

Retreat into the Desert

The desert is always the place of encounter with God. Sometimes it is a barren and howling waste where the unprotected soul is set upon by wild beasts or demonic powers. In this situation the Lord seeks out the needy soul, redeeming, shielding and sustaining it in his love.[1] But often it is a place where God reveals his name, his glory and his very self as in the account of the desert confrontation with Moses. Moses was drawn inexorably towards the burning bush, and as the glory of the revelation dawned upon him, the very ground reverberated with the divine holiness. The voice of the Lord called from the centre of the fire:

'I am the God of your father, the God of Abraham, the God of Isaac and the God of Jacob.' And Moses hid his face, for he was afraid to look at God.[2]

Yahweh, as the God of the desert, was the source of Israel's understanding of both holiness and love. Throughout the Old Testament the vision of this consuming and fiery God of the desert was mingled with that of the loving, guiding God, who led his people through the pitfalls and aridity of the desert, in a cloud by day and a pillar of fire by night.[3] The prophets and psalms are full of a desert spirituality, a mixture of terror and glory, of fire, wind, storm and water. The God of glory thunders through the desert, and the same God makes the desert rejoice and blossom in a fertility hitherto unknown.[4]

The Old Testament pattern of desert spirituality was the background and context of the New Testament revelation, for it was out of the desert that John the Baptist proclaimed the Kingdom and Messiah. And it was in the Jordan and the desert wilderness that Jesus was baptized, anointed with the Spirit, and entered into victorious conflict with the powers of darkness. When Israel left Egypt to wander in the desert, God became a pilgrim with them in the dark years of their pilgrimage. He descended to them on the mountain in cloud and fire, speaking through Moses who was a type of Christ. He sustained them with manna, foreshadowing the Holy Eucharist, and water sprang from a rock in the desert at Moses' command, and continued to supply them until they settled in the promised land. St Paul expresses a comprehensive grasp of the unity of the people of God as he looks back retrospectively to those desert experiences:

> I want you to know, brethren, that our fathers were all under the cloud, and all passed through the sea, and all were baptized into Moses in the cloud and in the sea, and all ate the same spiritual food and all drank the same spiritual drink. For they drank from the spiritual Rock which followed them. And the Rock was Christ.[5]

The Desert Fathers

As the world seems to shrink in the era of instant travel and mass media, and as we are bombarded with the consequences of modern technology, there is an immense stirring of interest in the desert, solitude and in the strange characters known as the Desert Fathers. We turn from a concerned reading of journalistic and Amnesty International reports of forced labour camps and solitary confinement, with all the terrors of psychiatric malpractice and torture, and find a growing literature concerning the origins, acts and words of these desert dads who peopled the deserts of Egypt, Palestine, Arabia and Persia in the fourth century AD – at a time when the Church was forgetting its pilgrim nature and becoming successful and politically manipulated after the days of persecution.[6]

At the beginning of his powerful book *The Desert A City*, Derwas Chitty calls attention to the context of the Desert Fathers in the three characters Athanasius, Antony and Pachomius, who were, respectively, bishop and theologian, desert solitary, and primitive abbot. Sailing up to the Egyptian Thebaid at the beginning of his episcopate (*c.* 296–373), Athanasius was watched from the shore by Pachomius, hidden among his monks, and he conversed with Antony when Antony visited Alexandria in 338. As Chitty comments, the mutual confidence of these three was momentous for their own time in Egypt, and for the Church universal ever since, for to them, under God, we owe the inheritance of all that is primitive and best in monasticism integrated into the body of the Church. Pachomius' disciples remembered him saying:

> In our generation in Egypt I see three chapter-heads given increase by God for profit of all who understand – the bishop Athanasius, Christ's champion for the Faith even unto death; and the holy Abba Antony, perfect pattern of the anchoretic life; and this Community, which is the type for all who desire to gather souls according to God, to take care of them until they be made perfect.[7]

It is salutary to remember these three, for Athanasius upheld the truth of Christ's divinity through much suffering and exile; Pachomius was the father of coenobitic (communal) monasticism; and Antony, born about AD 251 retreated into the desert at twenty years of age when he heard the Sunday Gospel reading in church: 'If thou wilt be *perfect*, go and sell all that thou hast, give to the poor, and come and follow Me.' Athanasius was the champion of orthodoxy and a model of a gospel bishop, and when, through persecution, necessity drove him into the desert, he penned his *Life of St Antony*, which has influenced the hermit and monastic tradition ever since. The lovely thing about Athanasius' Antony is that when after his twenty years of solitude in the desert, his friends broke down the gate they found that his bodily condition had not deteriorated by his ascetic training, but had improved. He had not grown fat through lack of exercise, nor dried up from fasting and fighting with powers of darkness. Physically and in disposition of soul he is described as 'all balanced, as one governed by reason and standing in his natural condition.' And unlike pagan dualism which is ashamed of the body, Antony's condition is contrasted in his physical health right up to his death fifty years later when he was still sound in all his senses and vigorous in his limbs. Even his teeth were all there, though worn down to the gums – at about 105 years of age![8]

We could go back still further to the tradition of Jerome's life of Paul of Thebes, a native of the Thebaid, who is thought to be the first Christian hermit outside the New Testament. He fled to the desert during the Decian persecution (249–51) where he lived for some hundred years a life of prayer and penitence in a cave. St Antony is said to have visited him when 113 years old, and later to have buried him in the mantle which he had himself received from Athanasius.

Retreating from a Worldly Church

When the Emperor Constantine was supposedly converted to Christianity, the sign of the cross in his politico/religious regime was the sign of temporal power, and the Church was on the way to establishment. Christian society was becoming synonymous with pagan power, and as Thomas Merton comments, the men who retreated into the desert in reaction, doubted that there could be such a thing as a 'Christian state' – that Christianity and politics could ever mix to such an extent as to produce a fully Christian society. Their understanding of Christian society was spiritual and extra-mundane. He goes on to say that these seem almost scandalous views in a time when Christianity is accused of negativism and withdrawal, and of having no effective way of meeting the problems of our age. But as he says, it was precisely these men who did meet the problems of their time because they were ahead of their time, and opened the way for the development of a new man and a new society. Regression to the herd mentality is our problem now – and it is the inspiration of these old Desert Fathers which gives the dynamic and access to these fresh springs of vital spiritual life in which the life of Christ flows for social good.[9]

The Desert Fathers would not be ruled by a decadent state, and would not be passively dependent on the morals, values and policies of a state impregnated by worldliness, ambition, power and violence. They would not be ruled, but neither did they desire to rule, or act in a superior manner to ordinary men. They were eminently social, but their authority was the charismatic authority of wisdom, experience and love. They also had immense respect for their bishops and priests, but drew a distinction between charismatic and political authority. There are a number of excellent translations of the 'Sayings and Doings' of the Desert Fathers, but Thomas Merton's *Wisdom of the Desert*, is an excellent compendium with its introductory essay and selection of discipline, sagacity and humour.[10] Their socio-political views as well as their spiritual values are included, and it is important to note that there were Desert Mothers as well as Desert Fathers, and in these days it seems that women are responding in greater measure to the call of solitude.

Simplicity and Purity of Heart

Another mark of the Desert Fathers was their simplicity. They sought to reject the fallen, worldly pseudo-self which had to do with Adam, and through conversion and asceticism, know the sanctifying power of the Holy Spirit. There was a quest for direct experience, not second-hand authority. They did not reject the orthodox dogmatic formulations of the Church in the search for God and a perfect heart – but they did avoid dogmatism, philosophical pretensions, and technical concepts and verbiage which led to bitter theological controversy. They actually lived the life of a disciplined freedom, grounded in scripture and direct access to God in Christ. They acknowledged the guidance of the indwelling Spirit and did not impose one way upon all. 'What good work shall I do and have life thereby?' was one of the questions asked by a brother. And Abbot Antony's teaching is recalled in the answer:

> Not all works are alike. For Scripture says that Abraham was hospitable and God was with him. Elias loved solitary prayer, and God was with him. And David was humble, and God was with him. Therefore, whatever you see your soul to desire according to God, do that thing, and you shall keep your heart safe.[11]

Purity of heart was sought in the wider quest towards union with God. This meant a clear vision of the world and of one's own place in it, an intuitive grasp of spiritual realities, and an overflowing compassion. This gave rise to the basic, practical and concrete sayings that are recorded in the *Verba Seniorum*, the Sayings of the Desert Fathers. We do not find great theological claims of systems in these *Verba*, nor do we have great schemes of spiritual ascent or mystical treatises. Instead we have *verba salutis*, words of salvation, basic, concrete counsel for a particular situation. They are sometimes illuminating, sometimes critical, sometimes humorous, but always experiential. They lay bare the ignorance of the beginner in his desire to know and live the truth, the frustrations of those who cannot bear the solitude and desert, and they portray the almost naive wisdom and intuitive grasp of the Fathers, who are loving and compassionate, but also very canny in their perception of truth and falsity. What is *said* is not the important thing, but what is *lived*. And what is lived is the overflow of life in the Spirit. These words are not universal principles, but concrete keys to particular situations, though they have wider application and have become common currency. In the *Rule of St Benedict*, these *Verba Seniorum* are to be read aloud to the community, and there are monastic houses today which have readings from the Desert Fathers and from the *Conferences* of John Cassian which also come from this source.

Manner of Life
The Desert Fathers are represented by Antony; they lived a hermit life alone or in small groups, unlike the coenobitic monks who lived together in an organized community under men like Pachomius and Basil. But at times all the solitaries and novices would come together for common prayers and the celebration of the Eucharist. Following the celebration they would hold a sort of chapter meeting to discuss common problems and joys, and impart some shared teaching. Then they returned to their solitude, spending their time in prayer and manual work. The weaving of baskets, mats and ropes out of palm leaves or reeds was their manual work, and these were usually sold

in nearby towns, and there was a warmth and enthusiasm in the hospitality shown to one another and to visitors who were truly pilgrims. Touristy kind of people were not treated so generously. There is a telling story about some monastic brethren who went out to visit the desert hermits. The first hermit greeted them with joy, and set before them all the food he had. But that night when they were supposed to be sleeping, the hermit heard the coenobites planning to go from one brother to another, seeking food. So at dawn he gently sent them on their way, asking them to give this message to the next hermit: 'Be careful not to water the vegetables.' The second hermit understood well enough, so he made them sit down and weave baskets for hours on end, and then added a number of psalms to the already weighty liturgy, by which time they were really tired and hungry. 'We do not eat every day', he said, 'but because you have come it is fitting to have a little supper.' So he gave them dry bread, and a special treat – a little sauce of vinegar, salt and oil! After supper he started them into the psalter again, and kept praying almost until dawn, when they tried to take their leave. But he would not let them go, but kept them all that day working and praying, for as he said, charity demanded it! The account ends: 'They, hearing this, waited until dark and then under cover of night, made off.'[12]

So there is humour mixed with sagacity, and a mature wisdom mixed with godly foolishness, but always there is the primacy of love, evident in mutual forgiveness. Theirs was not a sentimental and effusive love – it demanded interior transformation, a restoration of the image of God in the life of the believer. They had retreated from authoritarianism, exploitation, manipulation and domination of others, but embraced instead humility, reserve and reverence of the person. You come across stories which speak of robbers breaking into the hermit's cell, beating him and stealing all that he has, and the hermit struggling after the robbers to give them something they missed. These stories usually end up with the conversion of the robbers. Then you get one of the Fathers rebuking some monks who were instrumental in the imprisonment of other robbers, the result of which is that the monks break into the jail by night and release the prisoners. Then you have an assembly of elders sitting in judgment upon one of the brothers, and the gentle negro Abba Moses walking into the critical assembly with a basket of sand, allowing it to run out through the many holes, and saying: 'My own sins are running out like this sand and yet I come to judge the sins of another.'

There is also a gentleness about them, masked by a certain naivety. One of my favourite stories runs as follows:

There were two elders living together in a cell, and they had never had so much as one quarrel with one another. One therefore said to the other: Come on, let us have at least one quarrel, like other men. The other said: I don't know how to start a quarrel. The first said: I will take this brick and place it here between us. Then I will say: It is mine. After that you will say: It is mine. This is what leads to a dispute and a fight. So then they placed the brick between them, one said: It is mine, and the other replied to the first: I do believe that it is mine. The first one said again: It is not yours, it is mine. So the other answered: Well then, if it is yours, take it! Thus they did not manage after all to get into a quarrel.[15]

Obviously that story needs to be taken with a pinch of salt – many of these stories from the Desert Fathers of the fourth century AD are of the same genre as those from the early Taoists of the fourth century BC, or from the Zen tradition, displaying a similar wit, wisdom, spontaneity and discipline.

The Desert Fathers did not run into the desert just to save their own souls, as if deserting a sinking ship. They knew well enough that they carried 'the world' within themselves, and that only by sheer grace and the sanctifying power of the indwelling Spirit could they live lives of love and holiness. They escaped the manipulating powers of the christianized world-state of Constantine, in order to discover true life in Christ, and then lived it for themselves and others. They had to discover liberation from the world in their own experience before they could lead others into it. That they did, and the challenge which a consideration of the Desert Fathers poses for us is the way to liberation, redemption and love in an increasingly totalitarian and bureaucratic world. Their very withdrawal from political manipulation was the affirmation of the politics of the kingdom of God; righteousness, holiness and gentleness in such a context could be interpreted as anarchy by political authorities. As Merton indicates, they were living out the principles of an alternative society.

The Centrality of God

It is also important to point out that although personal and immediate experience of God was a priority for them, it was not subjective experience which was the centre of their quest – the centre was God himself, and God alone. The consequences were both personal and social, but the one thing needful was God himself. If this is understood then it becomes clear that the Desert Fathers' faith was rooted and anchored in the sovereign God who burns with the consuming fire of holy love. Such experience of God has a gift-like quality about it – a result of sheer grace and not of merit or asceticism. Archbishop Anthony Bloom speaks of the Desert Fathers' lives as a response of love to Love – in the light of the humiliation of the Son of God, his life, his agony in Gethsemane and his dereliction on the Cross. Their loving response is the ascetic endeavour summed up in Jesus' call: 'Renounce yourself, take up your cross and follow me.' And in summing up their influence and example he says that their vision of God was so holy, so great, so possessed of love, that nothing less than one's whole being could respond to it. They had reached a humility of which we have no idea, because it is not based in an hypocritical or contrived depreciation of self, but in the vision of God, and a humbling experience of being loved by him. And they were wrapped in a depth of inner silence and were taught by 'Being' and not by speech. 'If a man cannot understand my silence, he will never understand my words', says Archbishop Anthony, and he continues:

If we wish to understand the sayings of the Fathers, let us approach them with veneration, silencing our judgments and our own thoughts in order to meet them on their own ground and perhaps to partake ultimately – if we prove able to emulate their earnestness in the search, their ruthless determination, their infinite compassion – in their own silent communion with God.[14]

Retreat and Return

When St Athanasius wrote the *Life of St Antony*, he set many men on fire with the Holy Spirit, and vocations proliferated, as a hunger and thirst for God was manifested. After twenty years in solitude, as we have noted, Antony emerged as a charismatic man of love and prayer, instructing other monks by his holiness of words and example. In the final stage of his life he retreated again from the pressure of admirers and followers to a deserted oasis near the Red Sea, where he died in AD 356. The lives and sayings of the Desert Fathers are set down for our example, and to teach us the principle of retreat and return as examplified by such a life.

There are special and particular ministries within the Body of Christ, and this principle of retreat and return is one which may apply both to our personal and corporate witness. Times of retreat into God as the source of our spiritual life provide a reservoir of prayer, love and healing which becomes available to the world on our return. St Seraphim of Sarov, the nineteenth century Russian staretz (elder) who spent many years in his monastery and in the solitude of his hermitage, said: 'Have peace in your heart and thousands around you will be saved.'

But there are some within the Body of Christ who may be aware of an unfolding vocation to a more contemplative life, either within a community or in solitude. The principle of retreat and return for them is more corporate, for this principle then operates *within the Body*. The members of our physical bodies serve particular functions within the unity of the organism. Some of them are communicating members, such as the eyes, the ears, the tongue, the hands and feet, as well as possessing other functions. But there are some members and organs which are vital and may not *seem* to communicate, in that they do not engaged in verbal or visible dialogue, but they have the primary function of sustaining life, and participate in the life-system in a hidden manner, and are indispensable. The heart is such a vital organ, though it is symbolically associated with the communication of compassion and love. The liver is such an organ which cannot be seen, felt or 'experienced' by the layman. It is a hidden and vital organ which performs basic indispensable functions, but is not thought to be a communicative organ in the sense referred to above. So, in the Body of Christ, there are those called to a hidden life, a vital life, a life of interior prayer which does not seem to have the communicative functions of proclamation, witness, dialogue or teaching. But their function is indispensable and vital to the living organism of the Body of Christ. The principle of retreat and return for them is lived out at a deeper level of contemplative prayer. They are called into the desert to give themselves completely in a life of prayer and love to God alone. Of course there are intercessory and exemplary functions, and there may be a hidden teaching ministry of counselling, direction, confession or writing. But the primary purpose is the love of God alone. And this is the tradition of the desert. Desert spirituality is radical, its essence is simplicity, it is for God alone, and yet it is for the whole cosmos. As Fr Roland Walls said at the symposium on the hermit life at St Davids in 1975:

> The eremitic life is in essence a grain of salt, a silent reminder to the Church of the exigencies of her life in Christ if she is not to incur the judgement of having become tasteless. The costly interiority of the following of Christ on his way to the Father must accompany the proclamation of what Christ has done for us once for all. The solitary gains stability in his vocation in so far as he understands the Christological and baptismal import of what he is undertaking, and that it is not for himself alone but with and for the whole Body.[15]

Living with the Desert Fathers
In the doctrine and experience of the communion of saints we are called to a participation with our brothers and sisters of all ages within the Body of Christ, in the life and Being

of God. When we pray, when we read, when we work, when we share – we thus participate in the communion of saints. If we could maintain such communion with the Desert Father tradition when making a retreat, we would learn by our experience, and our understanding would be an unfolding pattern in which the Holy Spirit who lived and moved in their solitude would make our solitude reciprocal with theirs. Referring to the Church's participation in the communion of saints, the hymn re-echoes our experience as we company with the desert army:

> She on earth hath union
>   With God the Three in One,
> And mystic sweet communion
>   With those whose rest is won:
> O happy ones and holy!
>   Lord, give us grace that we
> Like them, the meek and lowly
>   On high may dwell with thee.

References

1 Deut. 32:10.
2 Exod. 3:6.
3 Exod. 13:20–22; Deut 9:24.
4 Psa. 29:3; 97:2–6; Isa 35 *passim*.
5 I Cor 10:1–4.
6 References and works devoted to the Desert Fathers are both serious and affectionately humorous. The classic dogmatic book *Fathers and Heretics* by G. L. Prestige is endearingly known as *Dads and Cads*! Humour in the Desert Fathers is almost as much a tradition as it is in the early Taoists and Zen Masters. A sample of Desert Father literature:
Thomas Merton, *The Wisdom of the Desert* (London: Sheldon).
Benedicta Ward, *The Wisdom of the Desert Fathers* (Oxford: SLG Press).
Benedicta Ward, *The Sayings of the Desert Fathers* (London: Mowbrays).
Ernest A. Wallis (trans), *The Paradise of the Fathers* (London: Chatto & Windus).

Owen Chadwick, *John Cassian* (Cambridge: CUP).
Owen Chadwick (trans), *Western Asceticism* (London: SCM).
Helen Waddell, *The Desert Fathers* (London: Constable).
Peter Anson, *The Call of the Desert* (London: SPCK).
Derwas Chitty, *The Desert a City* (London: Mowbrays).
Derwas Chitty, *The Letters of St Antony the Great* (Oxford: SLG Press).

7 From *Vita Prima Pachomii*, quoted in Derwas, *The Desert a City*, p. 16.

8 Cf. Deut 34:7: 'Moses was 120 years old when he died; his eye was not dim, nor his natural force abated.'

9 See Merton's introductory essay, op. cit., pp. 3–24.

10 Also Benedicta Ward's two volumes listed above.

11 Merton, op. cit., Saying III, pp. 25f.

12 ibid, Saying VIII, p. 29.

13 ibid, Saying CXII, p. 67.

14 Ward, *The Sayings of the Desert Fathers*, p. ix.

15 A. M. Allchin, ed, *Solitude and Communion* (Oxford: SLG Press) pp. 51f.

4: The Way of Retreat: Evangelical and Catholic

Compatible and Essential

The words *Evangelical* and *Catholic* do not indicate a party spirit in this book. They refer to two basic ways of understanding and living the Gosepl which are integral to each other, and which cannot afford to exist or remain apart. The word *Evangelical* indicates the profoundly personal and saving experience of God in Christ, in which the Holy Spirit initiates the powers of the new birth in the life of the repentant sinner. Warmth, enthusiasm, zeal and apostolic dedication are all marks of the true evangelical spirit, and faithfulness to the revelation of God in scripture is basic to the evangelical perspective.

The word *Catholic* denies none of this – indeed at best will affirm the doctrinal and experiential elements of biblical evangelicalism. But there are the added emphases which underline the corporate nature of the Church as the Body of Christ, and an unfolding of the sacramental and mystical life of the Church in which the believer within the Body is sanctified, in attendance to word and sacrament. There is also great attention given to the corporate and personal life of prayer as taught within the Church's mystical tradition.

If the evangelical emphases are pursued with a neglect of the catholic, then the result can be a dogmatic bigotry, and an exclusivism and sect-like mentality which refuses fellowship, disrupts the unity of grace, and results in a proliferation of schismatic groupings.

If the catholic emphases are pursued with a neglect of the evangelical, then a kind of 'churchianity' develops which tends towards outward formality, ritualism and idolatry, a negligence of scripture and a mechanical attitude towards the sacraments.

It is a matter for rejoicing and celebration in these days that the emphases of the two movements within the Church are more and more seen to be not only compatible with, but essential to, each other. In retreat (when talking is allowed!), it is exhilarating to find Quakers, Catholics, Anglicans, Baptists, URC's and other Christians sharing together at a level of theological experience which transcends denominational barriers.

Unity in Diversity

One of my favourite injunctions of St Augustine is expressed:

> In things essential, *unity*
> In things not essential, *liberty*
> But in all things, *charity*

This may beg the question as to what things are essential, and what not essential, and we must not evade clear and disciplined thinking – but it certainly gives the right perspective for the pursuit of an experiential theology by which to live and pray, 'speaking the truth in love.' Love, poured into our hearts by the Holy Spirit is the basic, sustaining power which builds and binds the Body of Christ. As the apostle says: 'Speaking the truth in love, we will in all things grow up into him who is the Head, that is, Christ. From him the whole Body, joined and held together by every supporting ligament, grows and builds itself up in love, as each part does its work.'[1]

I remember in my younger, over-zealous days, somewhat mischievously asking a monk: 'What would you reply if I asked you if you were born again?' He answered with a smile: 'I would say that I am a member of the Holy Catholic Church of Jesus Christ.' That was a good answer, because it put my rather party-Evangelical question into a more apostolic and corporate context – and it set me thinking!

I find it a great joy to be able to speak to Evangelical and Catholic groups these days on the life of prayer, and to find that there is a similar depth of desire to go deeper into God with a cross-fertilization of insights and emphases. To find a Quaker like Richard Foster writing on the evangelical experience, with an awareness of the classical catholic disciplines, and with a commendatory Foreword by David Watson, an evangelical Anglican in sheer joy. I must say that I was relieved when the other day I saw a rather pious priest at our silent refectory meal reading a book with the emblazoned title: *Money, Sex and Power*, and found that it was by Richard Foster.[2]

As an indication of the joy of ecumenical ministry I think of the welcome I receive as a Franciscan friar in all parts of the Church. I find myself giving a lecture on Thomas Merton, the Cistercian monk, at a Roman Catholic House of Studies; then conducting a Quiet Day at one of our celebrated evangelical Baptist Colleges; then one Sunday preaching at an Anglican High Mass in the morning, and in a Pentecostal Church in the evening. It is the same Gospel which is being proclaimed in the context of an evangelical encounter with God and a quest to travel deeper into the love and truth of the Gospel.

It is only by such unity in diversity that we shall be able to become aware of the depth of each others' commitment to Christ. It is only by such evangelical and ecclesial sharing that we shall understand each others' perspectives. We are different by racial inheritance, temperamental make-up, social and educational levels and ecclesial upbringing. We may feel that the worship of God should be simple and austere with no decoration, ceremonial or colour to distract us from hearing and understanding the preached word. Or we may feel that all our senses – in the context of biblical and symbolic act and gesture, using colour, art, music, poetry and liturgy – should be offered to God in natural and spiritual worship. The former may accuse the latter of ritualism, and the latter may accuse the former of life-denying negativism, and there could be some truth in both. But there is a way of biblical and aesthetic worship which combines the best theological and spiritual insights of both traditions, thus enhancing the worship of God's people in word and sacrament.

I sometimes feel that if the baptism of a believer by total immersion were to be enacted in a catholic context it would demonstrate catholic worship at its best. And if the evangelical Christian could see that the practise of sacramental confession could serve, under God, to deepen and increase his love for God, then the Church would be the richer for it.

The Way of Spirituality

Recently an evangelical chaplain came to Glasshampton monastery to spend a time of private prayer and retreat, and to write one of the Grove booklets. These are a contemporary series, written from an evangelical vantage point, on worship, pastoral care, ethical issues, liturgical worship and spirituality. They have overflowed the banks of their own tradition, and are appreciated on the ecumenical scene because of their theological grasp and openness, and their spiritual awareness of contemporary need.

Perhaps 'spirituality' is the area in which we learn so much from one another, and it is in this area that the work of retreats is becoming increasingly productive. I just mentioned my ministry among groups of other denominations, but it is an even greater joy to minister and share within groupings which are an ecumenical cross-section from all parts of the Church – and that is often the case in retreats. The publication *Vision* is the journal, Anglican in foundation, of the Association for Promoting Retreats (APR). As I write, developments are taking place to co-ordinate the work of APR with its sister organizations – the National Retreat Movement in the Roman Catholic Church (NRM) and the Methodist Retreat Group (MRG). The idea is that retaining separate identities, the three should operate from the same centre and be staffed by a joint secretary/administrator. And as *Vision* magazine put it: 'This would be another sign of the increasing co-operation between the three groups already evident in the field of training programmes and shared retreats. That co-operation can be extended and deepened at every level as we witness to our growing unity in the life of the spirit.'

The word *spirituality* is a difficult one because we are really dealing with the manifold ways in which the Holy Spirit stimulates the Christian to grow in Christ, achieving the fulness of his humanity. John Tiller in one of the Grove

Spirituality series speaks of three types of Evangelical spirituality, namely, the Puritan, the Pietist and the Pentecostalist. I am very aware of my own roots and the tremendous power that Celtic spirituality had in these islands during the early Christian centuries, with its profound appreciation of grace and nature in the prayer, poetry and creativity of the Celtic monks. And of course, there are many types of Catholic spirituality. I write as a Franciscan, but am very aware of the great deal of work which has been done on the affinity of Anglican and Benedictine Spirituality.[3]

The Three Sisters

At this point it will prove a profitable spiritual exercise to trace the spiritual development of a contemporary evangelical Christian within the current ecumenical ethos of lively Christian faith. The Lord has a sense of humour, and the foolishness of God is certainly wiser than men. The joke is often on us, for over the centuries we have been erecting sturdy denominational barriers and ecclesiastical walls either to keep the saints in, or to keep the sinners out. The Lord has parachuted his way in and confounded the ecclesiastical languages. Writing with a delightful humorous style, Michael Harper, in *This Is The Day*, speaks of his own ecumenical pilgrimage in terms of three major spiritual influences in the contemporary Church.

He describes a family of three sisters whose names are Evangeline, Charisma and Roma. Evangeline is the evangelical movement which runs across denominational barriers; Charisma is the charismatic movement which has gained adherents in almost every section of the wider Church over the last two decades; and Roma is the Roman Catholic Church which was once anathema to him, but in which he has found a deepening of his profound, loving commitment to God in Christ.

Evangline

Michael owes his conversion to Evangeline. She taught him that it is possible to know God and that the basis of Christian life is personal relationship with Jesus Christ. Through her he found the authority and trustworthiness of scripture, and she was more a mother to him than a sister. He stayed with the friendly circle of friends that surrounded her, and though he was aware that there were other sisters, the worried frown on Evangeline's face warned him away. Evangeline showed him books written against the other two sisters who were frequently denied a place in the family at all, though as he discovered later, these pictures were often grotesque caricatures. Evangeline taught him a deep concern for proclaiming the Gospel and bringing others to Christ, and none of these things were denied him when he met the other sisters.

Charisma

In 1962 he met the second sister while working for Evangeline's part of the family business. The meeting with Charisma had a clandestine element about it because she and Evangeline were not on speaking terms. At times it was tempting to think that Charisma was illegitimate or at best only a half-sister. Michael found that Evangline's friends were not as happy in his company now, a rift began to develop, and he was treated as a renegade, his reputation becoming badly tarnished.

But Charisma imparted a renewal, a gaiety, a spontaneity in life and worship that he never possessed before. Evangelical faith had given him a quiet and restful confidence in the historical actions of Jesus Christ which was liberating and satisfying as far as it went. But charismatic renewal gave him a new confidence in an ever-present Lord who lives and acts in personal daily life. It was an introduction to the Spirit-filled life in Christ, to the love which casts out fear, and to a new closeness and openness to people that had not been possible previously.

Roma

Some years later, Michael met Roma. Again there was secrecy about the meeting, but in contrast to Charisma who had been totally unknown before he met her, Roma had been known from afar for many years. Encounter had been avoided because of her bad reputation. Some of Evangeline's friends called her a whore and some of Charisma's friends used to prophesy against Roma. But Michael found that not only was she related to the other two, but she was chaste. When the three came together in later days he found that they complemented each other perfectly and made him intensely happy.

Before meeting Roma, Michael had read anti-catholic literature, and had well-formulated prejudices and fears, believing that Catholicism was a force which was actively working against the spread of the true evangelical faith. Catholics were his self-appointed enemies – any 'nice' Catholic he met, he regarded their 'niceness' as a deceptive veneer. They were wolves in sheep's clothing, and he wasn't going to be taken in!

When his prejudices melted and he found himself increasingly meeting and sharing with Roman Catholics, Michael says that it was frequently with a frog in his throat and a watering of the eyes. He came to love those he had previously rejected, meeting Christ in them, and learning from the Holy Spirit through them. The treasure-stores of catholic life opened their riches to him. In a disarming biblical manner he says: 'The Virgin Mary has come alive and I feel I know her now, in the same way as my evangelical heritage helped me to know St Paul.' God's creation, gifts of creativity, nature and nature's art all came to life, and the Church corporate, with its pre-Reformation riches, took on new meaning. The sacraments were no longer lifeless mechanical rites, but effectual signs that work where there is faith. Since meeting Roma, holy communion became an oasis in a parched desert.

A Fourth Sister: Orthodoxa

Michael also adds that he is aware that the family is not complete without a fourth sister – namely Orthodoxa – meaning Eastern Orthodoxy. He feels that the rest of the family seems incomplete without her. But his life has been so busy cultivating friendship with the other three sisters that he has hardly had opportunity to meet her. He looks forward to a continuing work of the Holy Spirit that will bring Orthodoxa into close relationship, enriching and sharing openly with her other sisters, for 'there is one body and one Spirit . . . one Lord, one faith, one baptism, one

God and Father of us all, who is above all and through all and in all.'[4]

One Family

In the new dimension of love to which Michael Harper bears joyful witness he speaks of his longing to see the full participation of all the sisters in the one family:

They are large spiritual bodies, which are at the moment pursuing separate courses. I owe a great debt of gratitude to all three. To the Evangelical sister for teaching me the Gospel and introducing me to Jesus Christ. To the Pentecostal sister for helping me to experience the spiritual dynamic of the Holy Spirit's activity in the Church and the world. To the Catholic sister for ushering me into a whole new world especially to understand the more corporate dimensions of Christian life and to balance the spiritual with the human aspects of Christian truth, the Cross and the Incarnation, Word and Sacraments.

I must confess to a deep longing to see these sisters reconciled to each other; to see them united in Christ and the Spirit, learning from one another and humbly listening to each other. If these sisters could be brought together on a large scale, there is no knowing the blessings that could follow.

Eastern Orthodoxy

Michael Harper's book was written in the late 1970s, and no doubt he currently rejoices in his introduction to Orthodoxa. The riches of Eastern Christendom are becoming increasingly available to the Western Church, not only in theological literature of a profoundly spiritual character, but also in the recording and liturgical use of Orthodox music and chant. But it is not sufficient to read about Orthodoxy, nor yet to use its musical and liturgical riches in a western context – one must be exposed to Orthodox worship, for it is there that the feeling of *sobornost*, deep, loving fellowship, is encountered. Orthodox worship has been described as heaven upon earth, the celebration of the eternal kingdom of God in the here and now of divine worship. Orthodoxy does not, with pietistic Protestantism and much Western Catholicism, gaze overmuch on a Christ in agony upon the Cross, but glorifies the risen Christ as the Pantokrator, the Almighty One. On Good Friday the Orthodox Church thinks not simply of Christ's suffering humanity, but of the pain and glory of his divinity:

Today is hanged upon the tree
   He who hanged the earth in the midst of the waters.
A crown of thorns crowns him
   Who is the king of the angels.
He is wrapped about with the purple of mockery
   Who wraps the heaven in clouds.[5]

Three Orthodox Presuppositions

The Orthodox Way is the title of a paperback by Fr Kallistos Ware which I endeavour to put into the hands of novices and others who look for some spiritual direction. It is a book full of theology and prayer, but readable and practical, spiritual and devotional. It could well form the basis of a retreat, and itself shows a creative mingling of the evangelical, catholic and orthodox elements in a fulness of theological participation. In the middle of an illuminating chapter on prayer, Fr Ware speaks of three indispensable elements presupposed at every point on the spiritual Way. Anyone who mixes with Christians of other traditions in retreat will soon become aware experientially, of these three elements, because they will be part and parcel of his own evolving Christian experience, part of the spiritual Way.

The first presupposition is *ecclesial* – that the believer is a member of the Church of Christ. The Orthodox tradition is not so concerned with the hierarchical or organizational structure of the Church as with its theology and spirituality. As Aleksei Khomiakov says:

No one is saved alone. He who is saved is saved in the Church, as a member of her and in union with all her other members. If anyone believes, he is in the communion of faith; if he loves, he is in the communion of love; if he prays, he is in the communion of prayer.[6]

85

There are many who reject the way the professing Church proclaims Christ, and many who have never heard the Gospel, yet who are true servants of the Lord in the depths of their hearts and in their manner of life. God is able to save those who in this life have not given their allegiance to the Church, but as Fr Ware points out: ' . . . looking at the matter from *our* side, this does not entitle any of us to say, "The Church is unnecessary for me." There is no spiritual elite who have no need of the Church, for the hermit in the desert is as much a churchman as a worker in the city, for the Body of Christ is one family.

The second presupposition is *sacramental*. Sacramental life, beginning in baptism, continuing in the life-giving Eucharist, is essential to every Christian. God may not be bound to the sacraments, but we are – for the good of our souls. For Orthodoxy, the whole created order becomes sacramental, as in the Celtic Church. Reading Fr Ware on this point reminds me of my first reading of Alexander Schmemann's *The World as Sacrament*, in which he sees the whole world as the sacrament of communion with God, so that the very life of God pulses throughout the created order, and nature is shot through with grace.[7]

But the spiritual Way is not only ecclesial and sacramental, it is also *evangelical*. It is here that Fr Ware calls attention to the biblical nature of Orthodox worship and life, quoting St Antony of Egypt when he was asked what rule should be kept to please God. His response was:

Wherever you go, have God always before your eyes; in whatever you do or say, have an example from the Holy Scriptures; and whatever place in which you dwell, do not be quick to move elsewhere. Keep these three things and you will live.[8]

Metropolitan Philaret of Moscow maintains: 'The only pure and all-sufficient source of the doctrines of the faith is the revealed Word of God, contained in the Holy Scriptures.' And the instructions given to novices upon entry into the monastic life are the same as for ordinary Orthodox believers:

From his first entry into the monastery a monk should devote all possible care and attention to the reading of the Holy Gospel. He should study the Gospel so closely that it is always present in his memory. At every moral decision he takes, for every act, for every thought, he should always have ready in his memory the teaching of the Gospel. . . . Keep on studying the Gospel until the end of your life. Never stop. Do not think that you know it enough, even if you know it all by heart.[9]

In the Orthodox tradition scripture is not merely a collection of historical and theological documents open to source, form and redaction criticism, though they have some place, but it is the book of the Church, containing God's Word. The Bible is not to be read in a private or individualistic manner in isolation, but in communion with Christians down the ages and across the world. Scripture is not interpreted by private understanding but according to the mind of the Church. The disciplines of study and the nurturing of faith are combined in Fr Ware's evangelical evaluation:

As we read the Bible, we are all the time gathering information, wrestling with the sense of obscure sentences, comparing and analysing. But this is secondary. The real purpose of Bible study is much more than this – to feed our love for Christ, to kindle our hearts into prayer, and to provide us with guidance in our personal life. The study of words should give place to an immediate dialogue with the living Word himself. 'Whenever you read the Gospel,' says St Tikhon of Zadonsk, 'Christ himself is speaking to you. And while you read, you are praying and talking with him.'[10]

Church, sacraments, scripture – these are the three elements which are the presuppositions for traversing the spiritual Way, and it is refreshing to listen to the Orthodox tradition as it explores these dimensions of faith.

Coming Together
We have spoken of the Evangelical, the Catholic and the Orthodox traditions. But it is not enough to be aware of

the whole Christian family, or even to read ecumenical and spiritual literature. It is our privilege and duty to meet – to discover and be exposed to each other across the great traditions. We can do this by visiting each other's churches, participating in each other's liturgy, but there is another way which I am commending throughout this book – the way of Retreat.

In making a retreat, and choosing wisely, there is the possibility of sharing a liturgy, culture and life-style that is not one's own tradition, but equally valid as Christian life and worship. A retreat under the auspices of the Fellowship of St Alban and St Sergius will promote Anglican-Orthodox sharing. In the pages of *Vision* one can select the particular retreat to meet one's own needs, quite apart from private and parochial retreats. There are many retreats which encourage spiritual encounter between Christians of varying traditions, while looking towards the centre – Christ himself.

References
1 Ephes. 4:15, 16.
2 Richard Foster, *Celebration of Discipline* (London: Hodder); *Freedom of Simplicity* (London: SPCK).
3 See Esther de Waal, *Seeking God: The Way of St Benedict* (London: Collins, Fount).
4 Ephes. 4:4–6.
5 This theme is expounded in Timothy Ware, *The Orthodox Church* (Harmondsworth: Penguin), pp. 230 ff.
6 Quoted in Kallistos Ware, *The Orthodox Way*, p. 144.
7 Schmemann, op. cit. Ultimately, Orthodoxy sees the sacramental life and uncreated energies of God fully permeating the whole Church, overflowing into the created order in the *Parousia* or coming of Christ in glory. See also Vladimir Lossky, *The Mystical Theology of the Eastern Church* (London: James Clarke), p. 235.
8 Quoted in *The Orthodox Way*, p. 146f.
9 ibid., p. 147.
10 ibid., p. 148.

5: What People Say

If I did nothing else but remain here in the monastery, praying and ministering to guests and retreatants, there would be more than enough to fill the available time. Talking to one of our first-time retreatants yesterday, he told me that as a lecturer he works with two particular colleagues who greatly impress him. One is an orthodox Jew who attends synagogue every morning and evening, and the other is a devout Muslim who prays five times a day, keeping his prayer-mat in his office. This retreatant is soaking up the atmosphere of prayer here, and is finding great joy in spending time each day picking raspberries, gooseberries and blackcurrants, while I make the jam! Another guest who is returning home today, from a strong evangelical tradition, has become even more aware of his restlessness, anxiety and feelings of guilt, covered over by an activism which has come to light during the days he has spent with us. We have not seen the last of him.

I want to include in this chapter some of the first-hand responses of retreatants who have spent some time at Glasshampton during the last year. These could be multiplied many times if I turned to our other friaries or to houses of other Orders. What I record here is a result of conversations, letters, or the spiritual journals of those who have shared their personal pilgrimage, and the material is offered with their permission.

The power of such a place of prayer as this has become evident even since I wrote the last paragraph. One of our Franciscan brothers came for prayer and a blessing as he travels north to look at a new ministry of prayer in the midst of a violent city. Before he came I wrote a card for him, and the words were so clearly God's word to his soul. As he knelt with me in prayer, and as we shared our vision of dwelling deeper in God and reaching out to human need, tears began to flow, and the Lord was there. He has just left, after blessedly interrupting this page, and he carries the card on which I had written the words of Margery Kempe concerning Lady Julian of Norwich: 'When God visits a creature with tears of contrition, devotion and compassion, he may and ought to believe that the Holy Spirit is in his soul.' And so Brother B goes on his way in tears and joy.

Unpacking, Unwinding, Acceptance
Ronald writes of his first retreat a month ago:

So far as preparation was concerned, it consisted mainly, in my case, of *unpacking* for the journey. I emptied out the bag which contained my list of things to do or to worry about for next week, and the list of things of last week which I felt guilty or resentful about.

As a practical step, I left home the day before I was due to arrive at Glasshampton, and stayed the night in Worcester without booking a room in advance. That meant that I was more than usually detached from the normal routine by which I know each day where I shall be sleeping that night. I travelled by public transport – I have no car – and I packed the minimum, and used a rucksack instead of a suitcase so that I could walk from Worcester.

My main impressions of Glasshampton were of a community, of simplicity, and of integrity. A community quiet and active, absorbed but certainly not self-absorbed, open to the world and conscious of and in touch with its sadder and harsher realities. A totally unforced cheerfulness and a hospitality which embraced old friends, new visitors and passing chaffinches with an equal and unsentimental warmth.

Of simplicity in the sense that there were none of the distractions of radio and television, that quiet was the prevailing environment, and that the day consisted of prayer, of helping things to grow, of study and of sleep. (The food was plain, good and plentiful!)

Of integrity in a unity of purpose for each day, which led on into the next in a way which we have lost in the fractured and fragmented life we have created for ourselves in our cities. The sentence in the service of Compline which draws out this oneness talks of awaiting the Lord's coming with the next day's dawning.

Release from Pressure

Alistair has spent extended periods of time with us over the past ten years or so, and his experience is not confined to one friary and to one set of brothers. He is a man of great creativity and sensitivity and life has not been easy for him. He has increasingly found spiritual and mental strength and renewal in prayer and sharing our life, and his sense of joy and gratitude to God is clear in his description:

One of the first things I have noticed about going to stay with SSF is the immediate release from pressure. Everything about the place and the people suggests that you should relax. After your first visit you know that you are assured of a genuinely warm and friendly welcome, and you can ease up as though you were returning home.

There are several reasons why this should be so. One is the quietness and tranquillity of the surroundings. There are no trains or streams of traffic to crash through your consciousness, and you notice birdsong as you may not have done for years. It is a chance to gain, if only temporarily, the natural sound of life which our ancestors were able to take for granted.

In this setting it is natural as well as gratifying to slow down. For a while you are out of the frantic tumult which is modern living. There is time to begin to notice things: the stillness of cows in a field, or the shape and texture of a mug you are washing. Life ceases to be something to be got through at all costs, if necessary at the expense of sensory experience, thought, feeling and sensitivity.

At Hilfield and Glasshampton the need to struggle for survival is removed. You are expected to work, but if you feel unable to do so, you will be looked after just the same. The 'standard of living' is modest and there is no need to worry about mortgages, bills, car repairs, television rentals and the rest. All the ridiculous complexities and luxuries which we consider necessary for life, and for which we forfeit our lives, are absent. There is only a delightfully simple daily round.

In this atmosphere you can rediscover the essential goodness of routine allied to ritual. There is a quiet, though far from monotonous regularity about this sort of life, punctuated periodically by the bell summoning the brothers to prayer. I cannot help feeling that this is how we are meant to live, performing essential tasks for and with one another in an amiable though disciplined manner. Routine, properly understood, tends to free the mind or spirit for creativity. Ritual gives a focus for and expression to its inherent sense of purpose and meaning.

Some of our houses are in the midst of frantic, urban surroundings and they minister just there. In some places we are in the midst of a violent community – the juxtaposition of those two words are incongruous but are part of daily experience. There we are called upon to be instruments of reconciliation and peace in a restless, purposeless and violent context. That is why members from such houses themselves need to retreat into God for periods of quiet and renewal. Alistair makes the point concerning a reconciling community:

Of course, agreeable surroundings and the absence of everyday stress are not enough. What is special about SSF is that it is a community of people trying to live together in love, and united by a common aim and focus. I sometimes feel that just as it is only other people who can do you real psychic or emotional harm, so it is only other people who can repair the damage. For someone like me, SSF is in the business of repairing the damage. It does so by the consistent practice of a love of which sensitivity, tolerance, respect and emotional discipline are component features. Also there is among the brothers a powerful instinct to seize on the positive aspect of things, however negligible it may seem, and to emphasize what is good while forgiving the bad. This tends to remove most of the harshness, ill temper and stridency one finds in everyday life, with a consequently heartening and mellowing effect on all within the community.

The primary thing is neither the running away *from* the frenetic world, nor the sharing in a human and accepting community, but rather the experience of that which is the basis and focus of our community life, the forgiving love and acceptance by God our Father. It is this that will prove its reality and worth when we return to our daily life and work. Alistair's long, healing experience prompts him to return for annual periods of retreat. And he continues:

This brings me to the most important thing I have found in living with the Franciscans. The heart of the matter for me has been genuine and absolute acceptance, freely and unconditionally offered. For someone low in self-esteem and confidence as I am, this has been a gift of extreme preciousness. I have found it scarcely anywhere else; and what makes it possible, of course, is the brothers' faith in, and love of, God.

Though deeply influenced by Christianity, I am not really any sort of orthodox Christian. My experience has been perhaps rather too pantheistic and mystical to be fully in accord with Church dogma. However, with SSF, I feel the presence of God in the sense that I know I am in the presence of what is good, true and loving, and what, despite some rough times, I still believe to be the most fundamentally valid fact of existence. I even feel a sort of right to be in an SSF house, an impulse to walk tall, because it is a house of God, and therefore no-one is justified in rejecting you. I have always liked the sentiment: 'You have a right to be here', and this is what I feel when staying with SSF. In a religious house, anyone who rejects you or abuses you does so at his own peril in the sight of God. This is not a point of view generally held in the world at large.

I remember leaving Hilfield in 1975 after a year with SSF. I took the train to London and in due course we arrived at Waterloo. I stepped out onto the platform and was immediately surrounded by all the hubbub and cacophony of a great station. In the pit of my stomach I felt, instead of the familiar sinking feeling, a deep warmth and reassurance, a strength, peace and steadiness I had gained by withdrawing to the Friary, and I knew I would be able to cope.

Hut Retreat

Stephen is in his early twenties, and lives in the east end of London. He teaches meditation to young and old in the centre of the city. He knows our Plaistow house well and has shared a great deal of his own piligrimage with me since his first Glasshampton retreat. For his second retreat he went into our secluded monastery hut which is provided for the kind of hut spirituality about which I have written elsewhere.[1] In telling me of his hitch-hiking to the monastery, Stephen said that he had seven lifts, and four of them had told him how they had changed their lifestyle so that they could have time and space to follow something meaningful in their lives, and he could see how their lives reflected his own desire to take a risk, change lifestyle and follow the inner prompting to love. But there was another side, as he says:

One of my lifts was with a man who was sure it was necessary to have a very expensive car to 'pick up girls' and that there wasn't really very much else in life other than sex. What I saw in myself in talking with him was how a strong desire can become so overwhelming (if I allow it) that it narrows my life, inhibits my creativity and becomes life-denying instead of life-fulfilling, which *ego* pretends it to be. It was almost frightening to be with someone so possessed and yet I see that potential within myself.

Stephen arrived at Shrawley, and speaks of the last part of his journey of withdrawal:

I turned my back to the village and walked up the long track to the monastery. I walked slowly, taking in the trees and ploughed fields. It's important not to rush this part of the withdrawal, to allow the rolling fields to reflect my thoughts and feelings, to withdrawing *to* rather than *from*. I am excited and apprehensive, this is my first completely solitary hut retreat. The hut really is a hut. There is a bed, a chair, a table, a gas cooker, and an icon – Rublev's *Trinity*. The only lighting is by candle. I will collect my meals from the kitchen oven and water from the tap in the garden.

From the door of the hut I look out to a field which has a touch of Zen garden about it, being very cleanly furrowed, as if raked. It dips down and plunges into woodland which rises up to the church on the hill. In the field stands an oak tree which I will get to know over the week. The light begins to fade and I prepare for my first night. I am tempted to draw up a retreat schedule to follow, but I see how this would be a form of escaping into something a little more comfortable. No, no schedule this time. This is a time of withdrawal from *busyness*. My only guidelines will be silence and enclosure, both of which I will break on Friday. This will be a time of allowing the silence to speak, rather than 'doing'.

Stephen shared his daily journal with me, and the sharing was an experience of recognizing in him a fellow-pilgrim on the way to the divine Love. As night followed day, and day night, there was a stillness and yet a development, a silence in which the eternal Word was manifested in his interior life. He gloried in the storm of the first night, high winds, thunder and lightning, with torrential rain. He dreamed that the hut was floating over the waves, and that he was separated from it in raging waters, but that a child was sent to take his hand and lead him back – even his dreams contained profound spiritual and psychological meaning.

He writes about the natural rhythms of the created order and of his own psyche, and of the spiritual rhythms of the life of prayer in the monastery and the Gospel of John which he read through. He speaks of sitting cross-legged before the Trinity icon and saying the Jesus Prayer. Like many young people today, Stephen was brought to a spiritual life through oriental traditions – he is a genuine pilgrim. He comments:

Something significant emerges today. I feel a strong pull from the cultures which have offered me so much over the last seven years. India and China and the far East, especially Thailand. Practising Yoga, T'ai Chi and meditation have led me into a faith not of any particular religion, but which is definitely living and breathing. These disciplines I feel have brought me to a sense of connectedness with the great spiritual tradition of Christianity, and have brought me here to the hut at Glasshampton. I feel I have to travel in an attitude of pilgrimage . . . to say thank you to the earth for giving root to the exploration of the inner life, of the cosmic life.

The Wednesday takes him back into his childhood, his longings for love, and a new sense of openness and compassion to other human beings. Thursday takes him by surprise, for there is a deep awareness of his sinfulness and need, but this is not in the sense of breaking any external law, but the law of his own being, his hearing and obeying the interior call to love, 'the love which moves the sun and other stars', quoting Dante. He comments:

Today the pain of my denial of this 'cosmic law' arose. I felt drawn into penance, and said the Jesus Prayer kneeling in front of the icon and bowing my head onto the floor in a posture of humility and humiliation. Today all this was meaningful, and I experienced a sense of purification and cleansing (well, at least the beginnings of such).

And then Stephen finds that as military planes fly over the hut on Thursday evening, he is catapulted into a kind of reflective intercession for our poor world, and his heart begins to cry:

Each time a warplane takes to the sky,
or a soldier polishes a gun,
The Tao holds her breath.

Each time a monk clasps his hands in prayer
or a nun kneels in silence
The Tao sighs with relief . . .

And the application of exposure to the whole context of
prayer and solitude is spelled out late Thursday evening:

Evening and night are very special in the hut. At home
I am very much a morning person, enjoying the time
when the city is waking as a time for quiet, rather than
the evenings. This is probably because the city keeps
awake for so long. But in the hut it is different. I sit
quietly with the door open, the last rays of the sun
illuminate the icon before sinking behind the hill at
Abberley. Everything around leads me into stillness, the
fading light, the birds' final chorus, lighting the candles.
All that disturbs the silence is the monastery bell, an
occasional owl, and the soft wind rustling through the
oak tree. I feel the urge to stay up all night. I understand
the night vigil now. In the stillness and silence of night
I am with the lonely and isolated, with the craziness of
city nightlife. I feel that so many things need to be
balanced through silence and solitude – the warplanes
preparing for war, people tearing around our cities mind-
lessly, confusion in relationships. In tonight's quiet I
sense an urgency for all this in our world at present.

On Friday there is an overwhelming sense of joy. 'If I
don't leave the hut soon,' he writes, 'I will burst with joy!'
So Friday is spent in John's Gospel, in walking, in a sense
of interior stillness. Then Friday evening is spent with the
brothers in their silent meal, and Stephen tries to capture
the meaning of the last few days:

In the evening after supper with the brothers I return to
the hut for my last night. Just to step into the hut now
is to enter into prayer; perhaps to be fully born is to take
the hut into one's heart. I feel I want to drink in the
surrounding countryside and the sky and the moon,
taking them deep into my being, so they are there always.
Maybe we only see reflections of our own heart. When

our hearts are open this is reflected in the sense of vibrancy and vividness in all we encounter. Although I haven't talked with the brothers we know something about each other through the silence. We are able to offer each other a warm farewell.

A Different World
Stephen is young, single, free and enthusiastic, and from him we turn to a busy married couple with children and demanding parishes to care for. Peter is a parish priest in his thirties. Celia is his wife. He comes regularly to Glasshampton, and then cares for the children so that Celia can make her retreat. She is gentle, quiet and sensitive, hardly speaking during a retreat I conducted recently at Tymawr Convent, Monmouth. From Celia's thoughts on retreat:

First retreat: Going to a convent – a different world, not knowing what to expect. Perhaps austerity and a cold holiness – but finding a humanity warmer than anywhere else. Fear! – do I exist apart from husband, children and housework? Is there anything else?

Private silent retreat: Four days without speaking – completely thrown onto one's own resources, and alone to God. No hiding behind potatoes needing to be peeled, nappies needing washing, children needing something. How can I describe the space it gives – the feeling of having been away longer than four days? The peace. Then at the end, a burst of light, of joy, drenching everything, singing through everything.

People say: 'What are you going to *do*? How are you going to fill the time if you speak to no-one? I couldn't do it – I need to talk – I need to do things – I need people.' It's easier to see why retreat is necessary afterwards – everything is clearer and brighter then.

A Three Week Retreat
Roger is an experienced priest from the Smethwick area of Birmingham, with profound experience of the peoples and spirituality of India, and a man of scripture, prayer and

communication of the Gospel. We know one another well, and he recently spent three weeks in (mostly) silent retreat, sharing the whole liturgical life of the monastery during that time. Last time he made his retreat with his nineteen year old son, but this time his wife generously packed him off on his own, while wife, son and daughter supported him in love and prayer.

Roger knows us and we know him. He is familiar with our pattern and rhythm of life and liturgy, and this familiarity was a good and relaxing beginning to his retreat. He felt that he could not go to a new and strange place for a prolonged period, and he arranged that no mail be sent on, and that his family would not visit. The seriousness of intent is clear in his words:

I felt it important to put myself under the authority of someone designated by the community. One was under discipline – even though it took the form simply of a gentle touch of the tiller from time to time. My conferences with Ramon every few days were also a vital part of the exercise.

I have always loved the worship at Glasshampton and one of my greatest joys was to be able to enter into it more deeply over a longer period. The times of worship divided the day into manageable bits and the psalms and scriptures commanded a deeper attention than they have done for some years. Somehow worship began to govern the day instead of merely being fitted into it. This pattern of worship enables each day to become a microcosm of one's whole life, and this in turn means that 'one man is all men'. The lightning of the lamps on Saturday evenings moved me almost to tears. All of us today have a need to return to the profound because basic simplicities which that ceremony enshrines. The worship, moreover, was that of a community committed to the costly discipline of living with God and with one another. When that is happening a community becomes a channel of God's grace for its visitors.

Roger found himself turning to the *Rule of St Benedict* which has shaped the lives of countless men and the whole life of Western Europe. Benedict led appropriately to Cassian's *Conferences*, aided by Owen Chadwick's superb *Life of Cassian*. Cassian was an exile writing for exiles after the sack of Rome, and Roger found in Cassian affinities with the Indian part of him. He recognized the danger of mere nostalgia, but in affirming the need to recover ancient wisdom, he wrote in his journal words of Simone Weil:

The future brings us nothing, gives us nothing; it is we who in order to build it have to give it everything, our very life. But to be able to give one has to possess; and we possess no other life, no other living sap, than the treasures stored up from the past and digested, assimilated, and created afresh by us.

Those last three passive verbs defend from mere nostalgia. There was a great deal of silence and reflection in the retreat, but reading and poetry were important throughout, and the text of the New Testament. Words Roger turned to again and again are from T. S. Eliot's *The Use of Poetry*, on the 'auditory imagination':

. . . the feeling for syllable and rhythm, penetrating far below the conscious levels of thought and feeling, invigorating every word, sinking to the most primitive and forgotten, returning to the origin and bringing something back, seeking the beginning and the end. It works through meanings certainly, or not without meanings in the ordinary sense, and fuses the old and obliterated and the trite, the current, and the new and surprising, the most ancient and the most civilized mentality.

These words helped him to get at the Greek text of the New Testament, avoiding the latest commentaries to which one can easily become a slave, getting at the text directly and prayerfully. 'In that way one can preserve one's independence of judgment,' he writes, 'for one knows which commentators are talking nonsense!'

The prolonged experience of silence helped Roger to see how much of his life had been governed by the demands and expectations of others, and by his own fears and ambitions. In the quiet there was the inevitable stripping process so that there was a new beginning, and the discovery of a new rootedness in God. This, he felt, was a personal experience of the great mystical tradition, and the words of one of the Desert Fathers took on new meaning: 'Sit in your cell – your cell will teach you all things.'

Inter-faith dialogue has always been important to Roger, and his loving and absorbed concern is felt in these paragraphs from his journal:

For the last twenty-five years or more I have been living, sleeping, writing, thinking, talking about the relationship of Christianity and Hinduism. I had planned to leave all that behind me for this retreat, but Ramon lent me a superb book on the Christian mystics by a Buddhist! Yet this proved providential. Two years ago in India I had a disappointingly brief interview with a Hindu monk in Rishikesh. I had gone to see him with my Sanskrit copy of Shankara's commentary on one of the Upanishads, hoping for a long session in which I could really learn something. Yet something the monk said has kept on coming back to my mind: 'Do you want to be a scholar or a *sadhaka* (aspirant/disciple)?' I had an uneasy feeling that he had seen right through me, typical westerner that I am.

I began to understand what he meant when I read these words of Basil Pennington on the fathers of Mount Athos: 'I perceive that I bring with me some of the restless urgency of our western world. In my contact with the Spiritual Fathers I am eager to get as much as I can. But in their practice they are content to give the disciple but a word, and let him chew on it for a time and then return for another . . . the Fathers are slow to give their time to the disciple, not out of any unwillingness or lack of openness to him. But they have engendered in the disciple this reverence and contentment with a word. And they realise they can better serve their disciples by prayer and sacred reading – growing themselves – than by a lot of talking.'

From my side, I must confess that the brief hours spent

with Roger during those three weeks were precious to me. It was not only a matter of tremendous rapport between us, but the experience of *koinonia* – the fellowship of the Holy Spirit and the love of Christ. We shared at the level of love and prayer and joy – and when Roger sent me parts of his spiritual journal some weeks later, there was a mischievous sting in the tail, for he writes:

> And so I returned to that pile of mail on my desk, and among it was the latest number of *Theology*. I read the article by John Baxter on *The Sangha Comes West*. The last paragraph intrigues me. Could one think of Buddhist monks visiting Glasshampton and the friars of Glasshampton visiting the Buddhists? To say more would be an impertinence, but to say less would be a betrayal, so I will shut up!

Roger is wholly committed to the Gospel of our Lord Jesus Christ, and he is also wide open to the whole world in compassion and enquiry and longing. This is the stance of a contemporary priest who, in the midst of our war-torn and godless world, affirms the power of the divine Love at the heart of all things, and is renewed in prayer to return to his task refreshed and empowered for service in a pluralistic society.

Personal Renewal and Social Service

More and more people are seeking personal refreshment, renewal and an oasis of tranquillity, in order not only to cope, but to communicate love and healing in our world. I have often met well-meaning people who suffer from what I call 'compassion fatigue'. That is, they take upon themselves, for altruistic, humanitarian, and often Christian motives, some work of charity, service or positive political witness. But they are constantly faced with pictures of starvation, purposeless violence, ideological structures and bureaucratic red tape, so that they become cast down with discouragement which sometimes leads to despair, and an abandonment of the task because they have no interior resources to cope with themselves, let alone the world's need.

When a psychiatrist came on retreat and humorously said: 'Lord, deliver us from the human race', he was really affirming his commitment to needy people in concrete situations in Birmingham – up to his eyes in clients. So what he was doing was learning, in prayerful retreat and humour, to renew himself, so that the peace and healing of prayer could flow through his ministry to the human psyche.

Peter is a fellow who is a child care organizer in Coventry, and the story of his life is one in which he acknowledges the constant need of such renewal. The pressure of his work is such that although he took a week's holiday from work to prepare for his Glasshampton retreat, nevertheless he was called in to three unavoidable meetings, involving the writing up of three case conference reports, and the making over a dozen telephone calls in the city's involvement in the reorganization of child care. 'I woke up every morning thinking about the problems left over from the day before,' he wrote, 'and any relaxation was marred by expectation of problems, and so free time slipped into lethargy.' The following week he left it all behind and came to Glasshampton, and in the middle of his retreat he wrote into his journal: 'Since arriving, work has hardly come to the fore, and when it does I have been able to acknowledge it and let it go, as one does with worthy, but inappropriate thoughts, when one is saying the Jesus Prayer.'

A Human and Healing Community

Reading over this chapter, it sounds as if we are a kind of exemplary community, radiating healing and light, fully integrated and well on the way to complete maturity and perfection. The fact is that we are a bunch of sinners, often not practising what we preach, not always allowing for the pains and trials of those who are coping with the difficulties of the noviciate, or of those who are daily carrying the burden of the many thankless tasks which are part of every community. There are times when we need to hear the words of the risen Christ to the church at Laodicea:

> I know your works: you are neither cold nor hot. Would that you were cold or hot! So because you are lukewarm . . . I will spew you out of my mouth. For

you say, I am rich, I have prospered, and I need nothing; not knowing that you are wretched, pitiable, poor, blind, and naked. Therefore I counsel you to buy from me gold refined by fire . . . white garments to clothe you, . . . and salve to anoint your eyes, that you may see. Those whom I love, I reprove and chasten; so be zealous and repent.[2]

The effect of such a prophetic word is to learn again that the condition of our acceptance and justification before God is sheer, marvellous grace! The basis of our forgiveness, reconciliation and healing is the person and work of our Lord Jesus Christ. That is why, as a Franciscan community, our whole work is to live and proclaim Jesus as Saviour and Lord. All our words and works, if they communicate humanity, forgiveness and healing at all, do so because they are words and works of Jesus in our midst. Our friaries and houses of prayer and retreat are hospitals for sinners, not hotels for saints! And we are the sinners, though experiencing the healing salvation which is in Christ.

It is from this perspective of total dependence upon the grace of God that we are able to hear and receive words like that which came from a recent retreatant, contained in a letter received yesterday:

As always, I enjoyed being in the company of SSF. My mind seems noticeably quieter and less troubled, and my mood continues to lighten perceptibly. I wish I could convey something of the continuing joy of feeling myself returning to a more comfortable and accepting state of mind: the sensation of recovering from severe depression and confusion is the most delightful I have ever known – I almost feel sorry for people who have never been in that situation and who do not know the incredible preciousness of psychic health. Being with SSF is the most healing experience I know and simply in human terms, which are the only ones I really understand, I don't think you and the other brothers should ever doubt the unique value of the life you are living.

If that quotation appears in this chapter, you will know that not only are those sentiments truly felt, but that the retreatant is happy for them to bear witness to his experience of retreat.

My own response to such words is immense gratitude to God, together with words which are found on the lips of Jesus, of his disciples, and of the woman who found in Jesus a Saviour and friend: 'Come, and see.'[3] They are words of invitation to the pilgrimage of making a retreat.

References

1 See *HF*, pp. 136ff.
2 Rev. 3:15–19.
3 John 1:39,46; 4:29.

PART II: APPLICATION

How To Do It

6: From Marketplace to Desert

Preparation for Interior Exploration

By *marketplace* I mean one's ordinary place of employment or the place where life is lived from day to day. For some it may be an actual site or activity of employment, for others it may be caring for house and children. For some it may be another aimless day on social security, while for others it may be a hospital bed or another day in the life of a busy doctor, district nurse, home-help or student.

The *desert*, on the other hand, may be an actual place or time of retreat in a monastery, hermitage or caravan. It may be sharing with others, having come away from one's ordinary occupations, or it may be a place and time completely alone in some dug-out, where only one or two people know where you are.

Of course, you don't have to go away from ordinary occupations to create a spiritual desert with its quiet oasis in your own heart. That is really what the Gospel is about – the finding of such a place of acceptance, tranquillity, prayer and love within the heart of God. Some years ago I had charge of a small church in Resolven in the Neath Valley where we used to meet early on a Thursday morning for prayer and rest in the loving presence of the Lord. It was a precious and memorable time, and one of the hymns we used to sing encapsulates what it means to have this interior solitude of the heart within the marketplace:

> There is a place of quiet rest
> Near to the heart of God;
> A place where sin cannot molest,
> Near to the heart of God.
> O Jesus, blest Redeemer,
> Sent from the heart of God

Draw us who wait before you
Near to the heart of God.

One of the advantages of this village was that it was a small island of people between Swansea / Neath and the 'heads of the valley road'. There was something insular about it, unlike the other churches in which I have exercised a pastoral ministry. This very fact encouraged a more contemplative dimension in me and in the people. Even going back now, years later, I feel the same rapport and love. While writing these lines I rang one particular family in order to check how to quote the hymn correctly, and the immediacy, love and fellowship of prayer in our Lord was there!

So the *desert* may be an inward desert of prayer and love – and ultimately that is what it becomes anyway. But in order to achieve this, and to deepen its experience, there is often the need to get away from the ordinary things, the ordinary place, and the often frenetic pace of life for a time of retreat.

In *A Hidden Fire* I told about a young man who spent a week in our Glasshampton monastery to prepare for his marriage – that was two years ago. Today his wife brought him again. She has spent a pre-Easter silent retreat with the Community of the Holy Name at Malvern, and has delivered him for a week of the same with us!

And also today I have had a second session with a priest who is spending three weeks of silence here, having together with his wife half a lifetime of missionary and parish work behind him. He has come to a crossroads and they are both spending a time of retreat and evaluation in listening before the Lord. It is sheer joy to share with him. He is at the end of his first week, and goes walking in the surrounding countryside every afternoon. 'This is the first time for many years', he said today, 'that I have done just nothing. I've been so busy. And today, just as I got to the meadow at the river Severn, I felt welling up within me the words: "The Lord is my Shepherd. . . . he leads me beside still waters and green pastures." ' Three weeks of silence, prayer and manual work is a good antidote to his workaholic past. His special work is among Moslem and

Hindu folk, and with his wife, who has a special ministry among Sikh women, there is a sharing of compassion in a practical and loving way.

At the same time this week we have a working theologian, a young married man in training for the priesthood, and a fellow from Birmingham who is an aspirant (wanting to join) our Society of St Francis, all sharing in our life of prayer and work. And together with these we have today a young priest and a young beat-policeman (young men in their late twenties) from Handsworth, Birmingham – both have come because of their concern about prayer and witness in that part of the city.

These are just the people who are currently with us, and there is a continual turnover of such people, professional white-collar and blue-collar people, and some with no collars at all! Those with dog-collars often need more prayer and help than the others (save of course, Mungo the dog)!

Practical Preparation
Having decided to make a retreat, the first thing is to find out (a) what type of retreat you require, and (b) what venue is possible or accessible. Types and places of retreat are referred to in the next chapter so we'll say no more about them here.

Having decided, written and got a place, you will receive notice of what you will need to take, directions to get there, and any special information. You may be staying at a monastery, friary, convent or retreat house, or even in a hermitage connected with such a place. Travel light, but take the basics: toilet requisites, changes of clothing, warm woollies according to season, stout shoes (wellies if room), Bible, pens, stout notebook. Do not take unanswered letters, transistors, cassettes (unless they are to be used specifically in retreat). Bed linen, towels, etc., are supplied, and there is access to books.

If you are travelling with a group or friend – fine. But otherwise, why not make even the journey a kind of pilgrimage? One young woman who comes regularly for a Quiet Day and counselling told me that she feels that the physical journey, and the nearly mile-long track is included in the whole day's pilgrimage, and serves as a preparation of mind and body for her.

Unwinding

Many people feel wound up and tense these days. It is not always easy to unwind quickly and lose one's tensions merely by changing places. There are some temperaments which build up more tension in changing places and entering new surroundings. Allow for this, and make your own pattern of running down and unwinding. Until you have a pattern of this kind, you will need to spend some time actually allowing yourself to shed your tensions and apprehensions. There is no need to be uptight and nervous – after all, you are in retreat from such! It should be a time of physical and spiritual passivity, together with a learning to create an interior pool of spiritual reserves. At least acknowledge that these things are so, and in other parts of this book and in the retreat itself, you will absorb the 'know-how' of relaxation, passivity, unwinding and tranquillity.

Temperamental Differences

You know how different people are. Some enter into new company, mix easily, talk fluently, enjoy themselves, and behave in a notoriously gregarious manner. It all looks so simple and flows so smoothly. And others? They are shy, nervous, apprehensive of new faces, lacking in conversation, unable to make small talk, unresponsive to questioning, and feel that they have no positive intellectual or spiritual contribution to make. But things are not what they seem. Those gregarious characters are often masking their nervousness, and their pushiness is often a compensation for shyness or fears. And the quiet ones are sometimes simply observing the behaviour of the others, or are gently and unobtrusively allowing the occasion to yield its own meaning.

The fact is that you are you, and there is no need for you to be talkative, knowledgeable, efficient, or anything else. Certainly, if you are new to it all, just determine, after some prayer and deep breathing, simply to be there. There is usually a Guestmaster/mistress who will put you at ease, and there are always more experienced retreatants who will help and share if need be. If you need something, just ask. If you don't know what page to turn to, which piece of cutlery to use – observe others. (The latter is no problem with us!) If you are on a corporate or individual silent retreat, and really do not want to whisper to a non-retreatant, then pass a note. But a simple rule would be not to break the silence of another person on retreat. There are usually talking areas anyway.

But apart from the social and domestic environment of a retreat house/monastery, there is the matter of spiritual attitude and response. When you are used to making a regular retreat, these things will fall into place, and there will be a comparative ease and familiarity with them all. But one's response to the spiritual and mental dimensions of retreat can be so different for different individuals, or for the same individuals on different occasions. We shall leave the deeper implications of spiritual attitudes and response for a later chapter, but at this point it is well to emphasize that the whole reason for the existence of the monastic or retreat house is that people should be drawn nearer to the source of their being, closer to the divine Love, and therefore in deeper relationship to one another. 'There is no fear in love,' says the apostle, 'but perfect love casts out fear.' Therefore the goal, if there can be said to be a goal in making a retreat, is to grow in love.

Openness of Heart
One thing should be said in terms of preparation which is essential. You will find in any monastic/retreat house, not only a variation in age-groups, classes, nationalities and backgrounds, but a wide spectrum of belief, from the convinced Christian, to the humanist, agnostic and atheist. And these days there are those of other world Faiths represented in our pluralistic society. This means that you must not set out to convince or evangelize others in your form of Christian (or other) belief. The monastic/retreat house will have its own Christian tradition, and scripture will be read, expounded and taught, and the Eucharist will be celebrated (probably daily). So your attitude must be one of dialogue (sometimes non-verbal), sharing and

learning. You are there to receive what the Lord has for you, sometimes through the group or retreat conductor, from scripture, reading, and other forms and disciplines. But you must maintain an openness of mind and heart towards others. In some of our houses you may encounter some wayfarers or a person with obvious mental and psychological needs. They will be taken care of, and will not be your concern at that time. If, of course, there is any thing or person worrying you, then a discreet word or note to the retreat leader/Guestmaster etc. will put your fears at rest. If you are a frenetic, active and evangelistic sort of person (parts of myself come into this category at times), then you must decide that this period, this retreat, is not the time or place for your interference!

Openness of heart and a willingness to listen and 'let be' is a precious gift, and it is often the Christian in the Western tradition (Catholic and Protestant), who needs to be still before the Lord and to learn from the experience of others who do not necessarily share his beliefs or life-styles. There is also the matter of a powerful and prayerful atmosphere of God's healing presence in many monastic houses which brings its own influence to bear upon those under such a roof.

Coping with Stress

One of the positive results of any serious form of retreat is that there is born a new attitude, a new vitality, a new ability to cope with stress. Not that stress is altogether bad – indeed a certain amount of stress serves as a stimulus to action, and gives a certain spice to life. It calls, challenges, and engages a person in dialogue, sharing and mutual inter-action. These are the positive uses of certain kinds of stress. But when we speak of stressful situations, we usually refer to those times or occasions when stress is destructive in its consequences. It is not that we are going to break through to complete freedom or deliverance from stress because we make a retreat, but we shall be enabled to cope if we practise the classic disciplines of the Christian life. And in coping we shall manifest a certain equilibrium and balance that is the sign of a mature person.

I believe in justification by faith and salvation by grace

– good works and ascetical practices must follow living faith. And if you live a balanced life of faith and works you will do more than just cope, you will live a life of victory and love. 'If you walk in the Spirit,' says the apostle Paul, 'you will not fulfil the lusts of the flesh.' At that level, theoretically anyway, it seems easy – it is the principle of the 'expulsive power of a new affection'. When a man truly falls in love, he will not need to go fornicating, destroying other lives as well as his own. But it does seem in our spiritual lives that the life of grace empowers the life of nature. We surrender ourselves to the indwelling of the Holy Spirit, and in his power take up the ascetic principles which the Gospel enjoins on us. The gospels and the epistles are not exclusively devoted to right belief and faith – they go on to make moral and ascetic demands. 'Make me pure,' prayed Augustine, 'but not yet!' So if we make spiritual affirmations and have good intentions about eating, drinking, smoking, exercise and right thinking, and then indulge in gluttony, purchase more tobacco, take no exercise, and indulge in gossip and slander – what's the good of our intentions?

This book is full of spiritual injunctions to holiness and spirituality. There are described ways and methods of becoming more aware of the reality of God, the Saviourhood of Christ and the indwelling of the Holy Spirit. This is the basis of a moral and ascetic life, which is then not miserable discipline, but enthusiastic joy! I believe a Gospel life should produce a joyful asceticism, but even the secular world appreciates the value of a moderate ascetisticm to promote good health and reduce stress. Let me here refer to the practical advice which comes from a secular Local Health Authority leaflet entitled *Coping with Stress*. It is a decalogue, and the ten points run:

1) Try and make sure that your time is sensibly divided between work, sleep and leisure.
2) Avoid the constant feeling of pressure and urgency. Getting up earlier may allow the day's work to be tackled at a more sensible pace. Allow adequate time for meals.
3) If you always feel anxious and tense, put time aside

every day for positive relaxation. This can be achieved in various ways – an engrossing hobby, listening to music, gardening, yoga or meditation.

4) Physical fitness is important in dealing with psychological stress.

5) Regular exercise is important. Try walking instead of busing or using the car. Have you started jogging?

6) Avoid smoking as it affects several of the internal organs, reducing their efficiency and producing serious disease.

7) Aim for a balanced diet and do not get overweight.

8) Alcohol is best avoided.

9) Set off for bed before you are too tired.

10) If things are getting 'on top of you', talk it over with someone, a problem shared is a problem halved.

What an eminently sensible leaflet to be produced by the Glamorgan Health Authority! I have congratulated those responsible. You see how well it is balanced between the positive and the negative. Concerning rush, pressure, tension, laziness, smoking, drinking, gluttony and overwork, it says GIVE THEM UP! And concerning relaxation, leisure, stability, creative hobbies, meditation, exercise, wise eating, sleep and dialogue-sharing, it says BRING THEM IN!

This seems to be what I would call *A Secular Rule of Life*, and things have come to a pretty pass when, because of neglect by the Church and its clergy, a secular Health Authority has to produce a leaflet for the physical, mental and perhaps spiritual good of its people. My attitude is to say thank you to the Lord for the intuitive understanding of such sensible people. Let us integrate all that is best of secular advice and counselling into the wholeness of our psycho-somatic lives.

I hitched a lift from a doctor from South Wales a few weeks ago, who had an extremely busy life, not only as a GP but also as a consultant doctor to the Royal Navy and to the Church in Wales. We shared some of the ideas of the above paragraphs, and he spoke of his involvement with the Westminster Pastoral Foundation. It was very good to hear from his professional life how ordinary, intelligent lay people are being trained in all kinds of pastoral and psychical counselling in order that they may function as centres of health and healing in our society. I spoke to him about the life of prayer at Glasshampton and the way in which people come to us and to scores of other monastic retreat houses around the country for this very thing.

It is clear that as our Lord moved about in his ministry of teaching, preaching and healing, his one aim was to bring *wholeness* to those in need. He linked the forgiveness of sins with mental and physical wholeness, and constantly ministered to the whole person. And he did this from a centre of love and tranquillity which was the fruit of his contemplative life.

It seems clear to me that as in every other discipline, unless one gives time, care and attention to the life of prayer, and unless one puts into practice some of the moral demands of the Gospel, then spirituality will lie either in the realm of wishful thinking or of downright hypocrisy. 'Don't do as I do, do as I tell you', is a counter-productive injunction. Unless our lives conform to what we preach, then it is better for us to remain silent. I remember as a thirteen year old lad, I asked a man I much revered to write in a book for me, and he wrote Emerson's words: 'What you are speaks so loudly that I cannot hear what you say.' I spent some anxious hours trying to work out whether he meant that my bad example got in the way of my good intentions, or whether he meant that my good example was valid even though I could not adequately express myself! The fact is that words and life must match up, and there are certain steps one can take to ensure this.

The laying down of a definite scheme is usually called making *A Rule of Life*. It must be very clear that this is a direct outcome of the application of the Gospel. It must not fall short of the Gospel, nor yet be an addition to it. It must conform to the Gospel, be a practical and realistic application of that Gospel to one's personal life in the Church and the world.

It is not my intention to deal with the matter here, but to refer you to the later chapter on 'Commitment: A Rule of Life', but these are the salient points to bear in mind if you are serious about taking your life in hand and allowing your conversion to be spelled out in a gospel life adapted to your needs and ability:

1) Take the Gospel as your guide within the worshipping fellowship of the Church;
2) Find a spiritual director/soul-friend to talk over the scheme you are adopting. It may be your priest/minister or a layperson.
3) Link your resolve with a definite group of people, certainly within the Sunday worship of your Church, but also if possible to a prayer or bible-study or meditation group.
4) If you are interested in making a definite commitment to become a Tertiary, Oblate, Associate or Companion of a Religious Order or group, write for the literature or go and see someone who has such a commitment.
5) In the light of the above, with the guidance given in the chapter on Commitment, plan and write out your *Rule of Life* to pass on to your counsellor for approval.
6) Let your commitment be sealed within the celebration of the Eucharist (as is often the case with our Tertiaries, or in a relationship with a spiritual director), or at least within the praying fellowship of your group.

Regular Retreat

If you are making a *Rule of Life*, then an annual retreat may well be part of it. In any case, it would be a good idea to actually go on retreat to plan the scheme. The whole theme of your retreat would then be a waiting upon God in quietness and trust, allowing him to guide you in your deliberations. One word of warning: do not be too ambitious and bite off more than you can chew. It is better to make your resolutions simple and practical so that you can fulfil them without undue strain, rather than aiming high with great and sincere intentions, only to find that you are unable to fulfil them. This can lead to discouragement, and such continued inability could lead to unnecessary feelings of inadequacy and impotence.

Remember that simplicity and humility is basic to a nature spirituality. Conformity to the Gospel is true freedom, and the yoke of Jesus is a burden of joy and peace. It is in the desert that you may hear his call and put your shoulder under his yoke, and you will be enabled to return to the marketplace of loving service with Jesus' words ringing in your ears and heart:

Come to me, all who labour and are heavy laden, and I will give you rest. Take my yoke upon you, and learn from me; for I am gentle and lowly in heart, and you will find rest for your souls. For my yoke is easy, and my burden is light.

7: Types and Places of Retreat

There are many kinds of retreats and many places which can provide all manner of facilities. I think of some of the people who come to the more monastic atmosphere of Glasshampton – they are priests, theological students, doctors, psychiatrists, social workers, youth workers, manual workers and unemployed – all of whom are in constant touch with other people. This place affords them peace, refreshment and silence. I think of some of our busier houses with a degree of social work and accommodation for wayfarers, school parties, camps and conferences. People who live alone or work in solitary jobs sometimes prefer such a venue, and their retreat may have a mix of silence, discussion, prayer and group activitieis.

There is increasing diversification in the classification of retreats, but the following kinds are available:

1) *Conducted Retreat* where a retreat conductor will give addresses, lead meditations and be available for counselling, confessions or interviews. The retreat may consist of a parish group, a Third Order group or a society within or without the Church. Or it may be an Open Conducted Retreat where the participants may not know one another at the outset. Such a conducted retreat may have a theme such as healing, counselling, and there may be more than one conductor. It may include participation in laying-on-of-hands or role play. It may be a fasting retreat with appropriate addresses. In all these there is the corporate element and apart from periods of silence, sharing is expected and welcome.

2) *Unconducted Retreat* where there are no addresses, though the retreatants may worship and eat together. If help or guidance is needed there will be a brother or sister available, but the emphasis is on prayerful silence and meditation. This approach is popular with 'religious' who

are constantly giving out and communicating in their daily work. The retreatants may belong to a group or not, but during the retreat they would not communicate verbally with each other.

3) Individually Directed Retreat, perhaps after an Ignatian pattern, which may last for a week-end, eight days or a month (or even longer in some places). Here there is a one-to-one relationship on a daily basis with the director, and it will often be tailor-made to the retreatant's needs. The demands made on the retreatant vary greatly in such a retreat – from a twenty minute meeting daily with a simple bible-reading and response, to a profound soul-searching which can be painful and challenging.

4) Creative Retreat which involves the bringing together of the corporate group and the individual in whatever creative theme has been chosen. For instance retreats of this kind are offered which include body-awareness, posture, walk, liturgical dance, music-making, painting, sculpting, calligraphy, poetry or spiritual journalling.

5) Private Retreat in which the retreatant lives in his own silence with God and scripture and plans his own pattern for the period. He may share in the life of a contemplative house in silent meals, liturgical prayer and Eucharist, but would maintain silence outside the worship. Otherwise, the retreatant might make use of a hermitage, hut or caravan in the monastic grounds, or may make use of a private place of this kind. Some groups share a hut, which may belong to one member of the group or be owned communally, and maintain pastoral care of one other in the process. The retreatant may use tapes or books during such a period, and may even go walking, jogging or swimming in the afternoons, though all is done with an awareness of the loving presence of God. Books of spiritual meditations and exercises may also be used,[1] but often scripture and silence is sufficient. As we shall later indicate, silence can be threatening, and one must be aware of the dangers. If this type of retreat is made within the context of a monastic or retreat house, pastoral help will be available, but due care should be taken if the retreatant is completely private, for one should not underestimate the dangers of silence and solitude.

6) *Home Retreat* with a retreat-director can be of different kinds and periods. It can vary from the spiritual use of a week's holiday for a person who lives alone, to a regular meeting over a week or month with a group who are committed to one another in the life of study and prayer.

7) *Quiet Day Retreat* which may be organized by a society, group or monastic/retreat house in which one day is set apart for prayer, study, meditation and reflection. Under this category may be included the kind of 'drop-in' retreats in which people can come for one to four hours, though the value of such a practice in terms of retreat is extremely limited.

Other Forms of Retreat

Many activities for longer or shorter periods are sometimes called retreats, though the term should be reserved for situations in which withdrawal with a certain solitude and silence is involved. We have, in some houses of SSF, an annual families' camp involving up to 100 parents and children in guest house, caravans, tents, etc., with communal, talking meals, bonfires, walks and hikes, as well as prayer, bible study and some sharing in friary life. Also there are two young peoples' camps each year, with some involvement in the worship of the friary. Individuals or small groups sometimes camp in friary grounds and share in meals and worship, but these activities are not within the compass of this book, and should not be called retreats, although the elment of withdrawal from ordinary concerns is basic. They belong, rather, to the holiday-fellowship/conference/bible and young peoples' camp category which is outside our terms of reference, valuable though they may be.

Places of Retreat

There are an increasing number of books of actual addresses and descriptions of monasteries, friaries, convents, retreat houses, etc., of all denominations.[2] Such books sometimes contain first-hand information of the writer's visits, though in one of them it was a bit difficult to recognize the glowing description of our monastery (no prizes given for discovering which publication!). Such books can be invaluable, though sometimes a real nuisance to monastic-type houses, which live in the tension of wanting to be available to those who seek to deepen their lives of prayer, reflection and study through the sharing of the religious life, while at the same time wanting to dissuade touristy kind of people from invading the necessary solitude. But these are comments from the inside!

Some of these books not only move across denominational barriers, but also include Buddhist and Hindu centres. There can only be positive value in learning from other faiths, though there is a whole world of experience to be gained from visiting retreat centres of one's own faith with a different tradition or churchmanship. Anglicans should visit Roman Catholic and Baptist centres; Roman Catholics should experience Anglican and Methodist houses; Baptists, Pentecostals and Quakers should be open to liturgical and sacramental worship – and so on. These are days of great opportunity and challenge to open our minds and hearts, to widen our horizons and to inform our understanding right across the board. How good to be exposed to Eastern Orthodox worship with its light, glory and mystery, even if we don't understand everything that's going on. There is immense diversity within the Church of God, and this is all to the good and will extend the frontiers of our loving concern for one another.

Holy Places and Pilgrimage
In the Old Testament there are many holy places, made holy by the presence and manifestation of God at a particular time in the revelation of his holiness and love. We have surveyed some of these in speaking of the biblical background to the concept of retreat. These are places to which, in later times if the location was known, pilgrimage was made. The temple at Jerusalem became the central place of pilgrimage in the experience of Israel, and from the earliest days of the tent of worship right up to the days of the temple of Herod, the precious veil hung between the holy place and the holy of holies, indicating a certain separation of transcendence between the utter holiness of God and the common people.

The powerful symbol of the rending of that veil of separation in the gospels at the death of Jesus[3] indicates that as our Saviour and Pioneer, Jesus has entered into that which is within the veil, having blazed the trail for us into the sacred presence of the living God.[4] By the rending of the veil of Christ's flesh the new and living way into the presence of God is made possible for every repentant sinner.

On the day of Pentecost, the Holy Spirit came upon the waiting believers gathered around the apostle Peter and Mary the mother of Jesus,[5] so that the believers became the Body of Christ, the living temple of God, made up of living stones. And with the coming of the Holy Spirit they became the living reality of what was typified in the shekinah glory of God dwelling in the holy of holies in the temple at Jerusalem.[6]

This is a revolutionary understanding of the Being and presence of God among his people. God does not dwell in holy places made with hands, but in the hearts of his faithful people, for they are the temple of God. Holy places are where the people of God gather for prayer and worship, and pilgrimage is not a long and arduous journey of merit to find the far away, transcendent God who separates himself from us, but a journey and celebration of love and faith in praise of the God who has made himself known to us in Christ.

Now if we understand this quite clearly, and have a living experience of personal and corporate indwelling of the Holy Spirit, then we can value places where God has especially manifested his presence, or places which have been sanctified by prayer and worship. T. S. Eliot captures the meaning of a holy place in *Little Gidding*, the last section of his *Four Quartets*:

>   If you came this way,
> Taking any route, starting from anywhere,
> At any time or at any season,
> It would always be the same: you would have to put off
> Sense and notion. You are not here to verify,
> Instruct yourself, or inform curiosity
> Or carry report. You are here to kneel
> Where prayer has been valid. And prayer is more
> Than an order of words, the conscious occupation

Of the praying mind, or the sound of the voice praying.

Retreat then, is to know and feel in one's mind and heart, the blinding reality of God's loving presence It is not to run away from the world where God is absent, to a holy place where he is present. He is the God whose centre is everywhere and whose circumference is nowhere. Retreat is to enter into a place of stillness and prayer, a place 'where prayer is wont to be made'.[7] The monastery where I now write is such a place. The word of God in scripture is continually read and meditated upon; the bread and wine of God in sacrament is continually offered and received; and the interior indwelling of God is continually experienced within the inmost cave of the heart. All this to the glory of God and the healing of mankind.

Made Holy by Prayer

It is a life-giving experience to meet in a place sanctified by prayer, having made the effort of pilgrimage to get there, and with a holy expectancy that God would actually meet and bless his people. Can you imagine what I felt when, after much hopeful anticipation I arrived at St Davids, Wales, in the Autumn of 1975, to share in a week of silence, fellowship and sharing at the Hermit Symposium, to hear these words?

I want to begin with a very simple affirmation. I believe that the question we have come to study here together during these days is one of vital importance not only for the whole Church, but for all mankind. We have come purposely to a place which seems marginal, and we shall be talking about a way of life which, in our time at least, seems particularly marginal. Yet, as I shall hope to suggest, the place of the solitary is only in appearance at the edge; in reality he is the one who stands at the very heart of things.

The place where we are meeting, St Davids, itself may help us to understand a little more of this paradox. Geographically today it is remote and inaccessible, an eminently marginal place. In another age when, however difficult and dangerous sea travel was, it was at least less perilous than travel by land, its position was altogether different. It was one of the focal places of Celtic Christendom, a centre both of cenobitic and eremitic monasticism.[8]

At that time I was a priest and chaplain in Glasgow, preparing to enter the Society of St Francis, and that week was a turning-point in my thought and action and is one of the most important milestones of my life, the repercussions of which are still powerfully active in my present and future pilgrimage. For me, the power, the holiness, the mind-blowing fellowship and silence of the hermit brothers and sisters of St Davids was reinforced by the pervasive holiness of place and history. This is substantiated by the fact that over a decade later, the reverberations of that experience are spelling out, under the guidance of the Holy Spirit, the pattern of my personal and community life now.

Many Christians find that their interior life of prayer is enriched by a pilgrimage to the holy land, to walk again where Jesus walked, to linger prayerfully in those places associated with his incarnate life, death and resurrection. And the people I know who have made a pilgrimage to the holy mountain of Athos in Greece have found it a stimulating experience of insight into the Orthodox monastic tradition stretching back into the early history of Christian monasticism. A. M. Allchin has a beautiful essay, 'The Way of Solitude', in which he speaks of the Island of Bardsey on the Lleyn Peninsula as a holy place, the island of 20,000 saints.[9] That also I proved experientially when spending my solitary six months facing the island on the tip of the Peninsula during the Winter of 1983/4.

The previous six months of solitude in Dorset in 1982 was on a spot which I felt was neutral ground – that is, I went walking one evening during my search for a place, and found this wooded area not far from our friary which had been untouched for many years. There was no feeling of darkness about it, and no intense feeling of prayer, but rather a neutral, potential feeling of welcome. After giving thanks for such a place, we erected a suitable hut on the ground, and before I entered the place for the period, the

Guardian and I did a Jericho march around it, with incense, singing and prayer, then blessing the whole area and celebrating the Eucharist inside the hut. I have been told from within and outside the community since then, that there is now a positive and prayerful feel about the place – it has been *made holy* by prayer.

The six months on the Lleyn Peninsula was not in a neutral place, as I have noted. It has been a Christian holy place from at least the fourth century. But the reputation is not only one of holiness but of darkness, for it seems that there were pagan sites on the peninsula and on the island in pre-Christian times. Certainly I experienced both these things. I did not only *bring* my spirituality and prayer to this place, but *found* both the light and the darkness which enshrouded the island and peninsula in varying moods and times. My prayers and solitude were added to what was already there, and even now, the *thought* of that place causes an answering echo within my heart, and calls to me from its solitude and mystery. Not only do I hear the heaving of the sea throughout those desolate and awakening months, but I feel the rising of the winds and storms, and see the painfully beautiful evenings of setting suns over Caernarfon Bay and the Irish Sea.

In a different kind of way I feel the effect of the prayers and faithfulness of Father William of Glasshampton who founded this monastery in which I live now, and began a contemplative and enclosed life in the converted stables which now house the Society of St Francis.[10] It serves as a contemplative house for some professed brothers, and novices spend eight months of their three year noviciate at Glasshampton, which also has room for five guests who share our life for short periods of retreat.

Fr William's life and witness at Glasshampton for eighteen years from 1918 were full of joy and difficulty. After the first four years he wrote: 'We stand for something no other community stands for . . . quietness, hiddenness and simplicity, prayer and labour and silence – nothing else.' He died on Easter Day 1937, and at Easter Day Evensong this year we processed around the cloister to his grave in the garth of the monastery singing a resurrection hymn, and gave thanks for his life and influence. Then we heard, in his own words, of his compassion for the world and his commitment to the life of prayer, ending with the following:

> God does not bid men to have recourse to the life of prayer in order that they may fold their arms and be unconscious of the sin and suffering of a distracted world. He never calls a man to seek his own salvation in ease and comfort, sheltered from the strife of the battle. And no man yet fulfilled a vocation to a life of prayer without bearing the temptations and sorrows common to humanity, and without a very real participation in the suffering life of Our Saviour.[11]

Every monastery, friary and retreat house has a story, and is a place of prayer and love. Father William is the foundation of the story of Glasshampton, and St Francis is the inspiration and patron of our Order, but it is the love of God in Jesus Christ which sanctifies, and his indwelling Spirit who causes holiness and love to abound. Making a pilgrimage to such a place on retreat, one follows the leading of the indwelling Spirit within the heart, and arrives at a place hallowed by prayer and sacrament, where the word of God is recited, read and lived throughout the day and night.

Interior desire and living faith are the prerequisites for meeting with God, but a place filled with prayer and the communion of saints is a powerful context. Confrontation with the darkness within oneself may also be involved, and the prayerful support of a praying community is a sustaining power in such a case.

References
1 Simple and basic books by Mark Link SJ: *Breakaway*; *You*; *Take Off Your Shoes* (Argus/St Paul's Publications); the excellent series of books by Antony de Mello, beginning with *Sadhana* (New York: Doubleday); more demanding but worthwhile books by Morton T. Kelsey, beginning with *Encounter with God* (Hodder & Stoughton), but especially *The Other Side of Silence* (SPCK).

2 George Target, *Out of This World: A Guide to Religious Retreats* (London: Bishopsgate Press); over 200 retreat houses listed and described. Geoffrey Gerrard, *Away From It All* (Surrey: Lutterworth); *A Directory of Monastic Spirituality* (Wheathampstead: Anthony Clarke). See also a list of Diocesan Retreat Houses in the Church of England Year Book (London: CIO Publishing), and lists of retreats in denominational periodicals like *The Tablet*, etc. Of primary importance is *The Vision*, the annual ecumenical journal announcing, describing, evaluating the whole area of retreats. This journal is a linking, ecumenical journal likely to become even more important in retreat work in the future.

3 Mark 15:38.

4 Heb. 10:19–22.

5 Acts 1:14; 2:1–4.

6 John 2:19–21; 1 Cor. 3:16,17; Eph. 2:19–22.

7 Acts 16:13.

8 A. M. Allchin, ed, *Solitude and Communion*, p. 1.

9 See A. M. Allchin, *The World is a Wedding* (London: Darton, Longman & Todd), pp. 107–123.

10 See Geoffrey Curtis CR, *William of Glasshampton*, (London, SPCK).

11 From the writings of Father William of Glasshampton.

8: Humour and Joy in Retreat

RETREAT: An establishment to which insane persons or habitual inebriates are admitted in order that they may be under proper supervision or control.

Humour and Spirituality

Living in a monastery, a place of retreat for brothers and guests, and then coming across the above definition in the Shorter Oxford English Dictionary, my sense of humour finds overt expression! I mean, am I insane, or merely inebriated? I've been accused of both – in the best kind of sense, of course, and I would be the first to admit that I am a bit dotty, and certainly often inebriated with the love of God. So the definition is not altogether inappropriate, and a book on retreats from my heart and hand is not out of place!

It certainly is true that wherever I have found people of great seriousness in their pursuit of God, and of great devotion and holiness in their manner of life, they have also been people of great humour and joy. This is true of the Evangelical, Catholic and Orthodox traditions, and it is a principle of universal application. Jewish wisdom is shot through with tremendous humour, showing itself with great courage in times of greatest suffering. Zen humour in the Buddhist tradition is renowned for tumbling arrogance and pride; and the antics and sayings of Mulla Nasrudin in the Sufi tradition have recently become well known through the writings of Idries Shah. The life and sayings of the Desert Fathers are full of the humour that deflates pride and gives birth to a proper understanding of oneself in relation to others and to God.

Humour is one of God's precious gifts, closely akin to joy, and if one is a Christian at all, then one cannot be humourless. It is to be treasured and appreciated and brought into all the serious and poker-faced situations which forbid joy and humour. When a Baptist minister friend came to Glasshampton monastery and shared in his first silent meal, he found that in the midst of the silence he wanted to laugh – part of that was nervousness, but part joy. He is used to it now, and as a family man, much appreciates the occasional silence of the monastery! He knows now that there is the freedom of humour within the silence. There are times, of course when laughter breaks out spontaneously within the silence of the monastery. One of the Guardian's tasks at Glasshampton is the serving of the food at meals. Recently, having decorously served the brothers with a beautifully sloppy spaghetti bolognese, I sat down in my place, and in doing so, tipped the whole plate gently into the lap of my habit. The effect upon brothers and guests was illuminating – from gusts of laughter to the understatement of an amused lifting of the eyebrows!

We constantly say that the actual life lived out in our friaries is much funnier than any *Oh Brother* TV series, as any perceptive guest who sees behind the scenes will tell you. But I am not talking merely about funny or 'ha-ha' humour, but the tremendous sense of play and gentle humour that is found in any genuine spirituality, and which should be found in any retreat situation. This does not negate the seriousness of the spiritual quest, but sharpens it, and itself gives insight into the nature and character of God and of his creation.[1]

If there is play, humour, laughter between brothers and sisters, then life will flow, and tears are more easily shared in times of pain and suffering. An inability to share joy inhibits the sharing involved in sympathy and compassion, and a humourless person is often lacking in other dimensions of his emotional life. These words need to be said because there is a type of person who cannot celebrate the sheer joy of creation and redemption, and nevertheless is incurably religious. Such people are found in all parts of the Church, and are one of the main reasons why ordinary human beings with rich emotional lives are turned away from the life of faith. Of course, you don't have to be overtly laughing, and certainly not putting on the mask of an evangelical or liturgical smile all the time (Lord, save us!), but joy and humour should be mingled with the whole spiritual and human quest, and especially in making a retreat. In such a situation, humour sometimes produces laughter, but more often a quiet smile of complicity and understanding.

Some of the Marks of Humour

One of the first marks of humour is a certain *childlikeness*. This is not *childishness* or naivety, but a playfulness, an innocence, and those who belong to the Franciscan tradition should know this as a dimension of continual experience. Franciscan stories abound in which humour and childlikeness go hand in hand. We see St Francis and Brother Masseo coming to a crossroads, unable to decide which way to go to carry the good news of God's love. So the two fools that they are, they turn themselves around and around until they are dizzy, and eventually find themselves facing in a particular way, and by the humour of God, come to the conclusion that this way is God's way.

Such childlike humour is devoid of that satanic gift of bitter sarcasm which eventually leads to cynicism and unfaith. How sad it is to find a person who is able to cut down another verbally, and cannot resist doing so. Such a one is more to be pitied than blamed, but what wounds can be inflicted by such action within the Body of Christ.

A second mark of humour is *objectivity*. That is, the ability to stand back and look at oneself in perspective, and thus to see how ridiculous is one's own seriousness. Such a person will neither be obsessed by his own guilt or arrogant concerning his own abilities, for he is saved from both by his humour which has its roots in divine grace.

It is painful to see how ecclesiastical institutions often take themselves so seriously with their hierarchical structures, clerical garb, unctuous faces and sacred cows. The garb, of course, need not be sacerdotal – it may well be a protestant pin-stripe suit. Alan Watts is a writer I have always read avidly with much amusement and profit, though more often than not disagreeing with him. In an entertaining essay entitled 'Is It Serious?' he makes the point:

When I was a schoolboy, we were dragooned into attending the services at Canterbury Cathedral, the Mecca of the Anglican Church. As we knelt, bowed, or stood in the courtly and austere ceremonies of this ancient fane, we had to take the utmost care never to laugh or smile . . . and very difficult to avoid because of the astonishing idiosyncrasies of the venerable clergy, with their propensities for bleating, whining, or bumbulating the prayers in sundry varieties of holy-sounding voices. There were rumbling Poo-bahs, and wizened little ascetics preaching with fervent shrieks, and between stands in pulpit or lectern they would process hither and yon, attired so as to look like rows of well-ordered penguins. . . . And yet neither the deadly seriousness of our postures nor the pathetic comedy of the clerics could quite conceal the atmosphere of luminous glory. High and echoing spaces of pale grey stone, enchanted with light that fell through the most intricate stained glass, predominantly blue; stone smelling faintly and pleasantly musty, like a wine cellar, and the whole building seeming to float above the congregation with the dignity and independence of a gull in the sky.[2]

The Anglican Church is, of course, often the butt of sometimes tasteless, uninformed and ungracious humour, but bad as it is, the Anglican communion usually has the ability to laugh at itself, its structures and personnel in ways that some other churches of more polarized views cannot. Sometimes one feels that God himself is amused by the Church's ridiculousness.

When I was on the staff of St Mary's Episcopal Cathedral, Glasgow, a great source of amusement was a procession in which the Primus of the Scottish Episcopal church – tall, lean and ascetic – walked beside the Roman Catholic Archbishop of Glasgow – short, plump and jolly! It was humorous – but the Lord turned the tables, for my most cherished memory of that Primus, Francis Moncreiff, was one Maundy Thursday at the Eucharist, when he removed his mitre and chasuble, girded himself with a towel, and knelt to wash and kiss the feet of twelve black and white members of the congregation. It was a humbling and glorious experience for all who participated. The Gospel was re-enacted in humility and joy.

This brings us to *humility* – another mark of humour. A man who takes God ultimately seriously cannot thereafter give such distinction to this transient world. It enables saints to laugh at the worst the world can do. I suppose it is unhistorical, but I can almost believe that when St Laurence was being roasted to death as a martyr, he was heard to say: 'Turn me over, for I am done on this side.' In sacred art he continues to carry his grid-iron, just as St Sebastian does not seem too concerned to be pierced all over with deadly arrows! It means that the real saints can afford to smile in adversity, to laugh at persecution, and to joy in death itself, because only God is taken absolutely seriously. You can feel the joy within the suffering as the Epistle to the Hebrews lists the sufferings of the saints, and the humility of the Incarnation of Jesus is personified in their living and their dying:

> Some were tortured, refusing to accept release . . . Others suffered mocking and scourging, and even chains and imprisonment. They were stoned, they were sawn in two, they were killed with the sword; they went about in skins of sheep and goats, destitute, afflicted, ill-treated – of whom the world was not worthy.[3]

Humility begets joy and a deep sense of humour. It does not take delight in other people's misfortunes – the reverse is true – but it cannot but smile at the pomposity and triumphalism of church and state on the occasions upon which they try to be impressive.

Another mark of humour is a certain *sanity and balance*. Sanity comes from the basic meaning of health, and one of the marks of the insane is a lack of humour, fun and spontaneity. There is, sadly, in our political and bureaucratic world, a sort of official sanity which is deadly serious and totally lacking in childlike fun, and therefore in humility. Thomas Merton has a chilling essay, ironic in its title and form: *A Devout Meditation in Memory of Adolf Eichmann*.[4] In it he portrays a totally humourless Eichmann, and comments that the psychiatrist examining him before his trial pronounced him perfectly sane. Such a man turns words like sanity on their heads. Merton paints the picture of a well-balanced, unperturbed official conscientiously going about his job which happened to be the supervision of mass murder. He was thoughtful, orderly, unimaginative (another humourless trait), and had a profound respect for system, law and order. This is not the sanity of joy, humour and balance, for as Merton says:

> The sanity of Eichmann is disturbing. We equate sanity with a sense of justice, with humaneness, with prudence, with the capacity to love and understand other people. We rely on the sane people of the world to preserve it from barbarism, madness, destruction. And now it begins to dawn on us that it is precisely the *sane* ones who are the most dangerous.

This is a concept of sanity that excludes love and humour. The humour which is an expression of gospel-joy promotes true sanity and balance. It may not be the wisdom of this world, but it is the wisdom of the kingdom, the foolishness of God which confounds the worldly-wise.

Monica Furlong captures this humourous sanity and balance finding it reflected in the contemplative portrayed in *The Cloud of Unknowing*:

> Gradually, as he works away at his prayer and his loving, the contemplative finds the difficult details of his life fall into place. He stops fussing about minor needs and disappointments and learns to take what comes. He learns how not to strain himself emotionally, and he abandons everything which might be a spiritual affectation. An element of gaiety creeps into his relations with God. He can, if he wishes, says the Cloud, 'have a lovely game with Him' . . . He even, in a way that would make Dale Carnegie envious, becomes more attractive to other people, because suddenly he is 'at home with everyone he talks to'.[5]

Recently, when I was doing my month's duties as Chaplain at our enclosed sisters' convent near Oxford, one of the sisters, who knew I had been hearing confessions, had been to the 'Cash and Carry' shopping run. She had brought back some cleaning materials made by the Italian firm RAMON, and silently passed me the scouring-pad label which said: 'Ramon all-purpose scouring – cleans without scratching'. I took the hint!

It is also true that humour adopts the *dimension of hope*. In the 1960s Tom Lehrer, a mathematics lecturer, became popular because of his 'sick-humour' songs, some of which were ironic but discerning. I didn't appreciate his style, but caught the feeling expressed in one of his songs which envisaged mass destruction, entitled: *We'll all go together when we go*. He disappeared from the scene for some years, and when he reappeared a few years ago he was asked about this song, and answered: 'I don't find it funny any more.' There is a distinct lack of hope in our world, and among some of our best young people it is often expressed with clarity. I heard a sixth form discussion on the radio today in which a girl said: 'What's the meaning of bringing children into the world when there won't be a world for them to grow up in?'

Throughout the Second World War I remember the humour which was part of the Welsh as of the larger British heritage, as the docks and city of Swansea were being bombarded from the air. Even now, when the elders of my reminiscing family get together, there are gales of laughter recalling the antics and conversations of those days and nights full of bombs and humour. But there's less of it now and some of our most earnest prophets are prophets of doom and despair, with a significant lack of humour. It is not my intention to play down the seriousness of the contempoary scene, or to lessen our dedicated involvement with it, but to affirm the Gospel which spells *hope*. And hope dispels gloom and fear.

This is another mark of humour, it is an antidote to fear, and as such is clearly relevant to our times. Fear is universal, and mass communications give immediate access to each new act of violence, bombing, torture and plague. The agony and suffering of the whole world is before our eyes, within our ears and beating in our hearts. There is a great danger of such fear giving rise to despair and complete impotence, and without the sure hope of the Gospel, humour would seem blasphemy in the face of such terror. But the saintly and humanitarian people and organizations of our world are touched by a gracious humour, for true humour has its roots in love, which casts out fear.

If humour has its roots in love, it also bears the blossoms and fruits of love. Where there is humour born of love, there is the freedom of 'letting be', of dialogue, of compassion and openness. This brings us round again to childlike playfulness which may be seen in the sisters of Mother Teresa ministering to abandoned children and dying patients in Calcutta.

As a little boy at school I was always struck with the kind of teacher who thought of our education as 'no laughing matter'. In our own childlike way many of us knew that this was the kind of man who could only teach by imparting facts, dates, theories, and we recognized the kind of teacher who could truly communicate because he shared his life, his excitement, his enthusiasm, and especially his humour with us, because he liked us – really because he loved us. As I write and look back over the years, I remember clearly the two teachers who embodied those two different attitudes. It is no accident that I think of the former as a man of bad temper, violence and injustice, and the latter as a man of warmth, colour and generosity. I only remember one sentence spoken by the latter, 'Remember boys – he who takes the sword shall perish by the sword.' He was right.

The human quest, the spiritual quest, *is* a laughing matter. It is also a crying, singing, weeping, sharing matter. Humour is in the whole mix of things, and its omission as an ingredient makes the product bland and tasteless. I omitted the salt in my bread-making the other day, and the friars knew! Humour is the salt of human intercourse, – remembering that there is salt also in tears.

Humour, Eccentricity, Madness
The old Methodist preacher Billy Bray was, like St Francis, somewhat eccentric. One day someone accused him of being 'cracked'. 'Cracked?' he cried out, 'oh yes, that's where the light shone in.' I unlearned a lot of seriousness,

137

and learned to express my natural spontaneity in joy among the classic Pentecostals. They used to quote with glee the scriptures which spoke of Christian believers as 'peculiar people'.[6] Their exegesis was at fault, but their intuition was correct. To be a Christian, in their eyes, was serious in the sense in which it had to do with the ultimate, with total trust and dependence, with the giving and receiving of the very life of God, but it was also to do with joy, dancing and holy laughter. It manifested itself in charismatic gifts such as healing and tongues and prophecy, in singing and dancing and rejoicing. Evangelism became the joyful proclamation of good news, and sanctification was the personal and corporate sharing of the person and gifts of the Holy Spirit.

In the Catholic tradition I learned that grace regenerates, renews, transforms and builds on nature, and that the whole world is shot through with the mystery and joy of God. Therefore, colour, light, movement, natural faculties of sight, hearing, touch, taste and smell were all caught up in the glory of liturgical worship. This meant that all kinds of music and musical instruments could be used in the worship of God, as well as the symbolic use of colours, flame, incense, charcoal, oil, water, wine, bread, and all our human senses. The worship and life-style of the people of God would therefore be criticized because of its spontaneous joy and splendour. For David was criticized because he danced with all his might before the Lord, and Peter and the apostles were criticized because they were drunk with the Holy Spirit.[7]

There is something about the contagion of the Gospel which infects the believer with joy, humour and a certain madness which is real sanity, because the foolishness of God is wiser than men, and the wisdom of this world is foolishness in God's sight. The whole message of the cross and resurrection is a foolish scandal to the merely rational man, and St Paul could write of the experience of the apostles:

We are fools for Christ's sake, but you are wise in Christ. We are weak, but you are strong. You are held in honour, but we in disrepute. To the present hour we hunger and thirst, we are ill-clad and buffeted and homeless, and we labour, working with our own hands. When reviled, we bless; when persecuted, we endure; when slandered, we try to conciliate; we have become, and are now, as the refuse of the world, the offscouring of all things.[8]

This is the way that Christ walked, for his own family thought him to be out of his mind at times, and St Paul was certainly thought to be quite mad.[9] Madness, foolishness, eccentricity have always been accusations made of God's people, not without some evidence! The effects of the divine grace upon some people have given rise to such spontaneity and uninhibited joy that it has threatened the circumspect and respectable, especially among 'serious' religious people.

These are the words of the mediaeval mystic John Ruysbroeck concerning the response of the soul to the touch of God:

Spiritual inebriation is this; that a man receives more sensible joy and sweetness than his heart can either contain or desire. Spiritual inebriation brings forth many strange gestures in men. It makes some sing and praise God because of their fulness of joy, and some weep with great tears because of their sweetness of heart. It makes one restless in all his limbs, so that he must run and jump and dance; and so excites another that he must gesticulate and clap his hands. Another cries out with a loud voice, and so shows forth the plentitude he feels within; another must be silent and melt away, because of the rapture which he feels in all his senses. At times he thinks that all the world must must feel what he feels; at times he thinks that none can taste what he has attained. Often he thinks that he never could, or ever shall, lose this well-being; at times he wonders why all men do not become God-desiring.[10]

Jacapone da Todi was a thirteenth century troubadour Franciscan friar, and the *ebrieza d'amore*, the fury and intensity of love, was his continual theme, enduring throughout his diverse religious experience. He discerned it not only in himself as a result of the divine movement of God within his own soul, but at the very heart of the created order. It was a sort of mutual madness, the folly of unmeasured Love, and to surrender himself to the ecstatic dance of Love was part of the sheer joy of creation:[11]

> For since God's wisdom, though so great,
>   Is all intoxicate with love,
> Shall mine not be inebriate?
>   And so be like my Lord above?
> No greater honour can I prove
>   Than sharing His insanity.

Of course, this is not an invitation to disordered and undisciplined inebriation. In all the theologians and mystics worth their salt there is the tremendous vitality of spontaneity, and the powerful asceticism of discipline. I have introduced this theme of humour and joy into the work of making a retreat, for without it, one cannot face the inevitable darkness of conflict, or truly enter into the joyful dimension of gospel life. It moves from humour and joy, into foolishness and madness, and back to a humour based in a simple acceptance of one's humanity.

Let me conclude this chapter with a story from our own noviciate training. The noviciate lasts at least three years, and during that time there is a honeymoon period of joy and sharing, and a long and sometimes difficult time of realizing and facing up to the demands of such a life. Of necessity there must be a mingling of humour and joy in God as one travels through this experience, otherwise one is laying up a store of repression and depression that plays havoc with one's own (and the community's) emotional life in years to come.

Brother J came up to me one day and said: 'There's something wrong with me; I'm all up-tight and I don't seem to have any freedom or joy – what can I do about it?' It was not the right time to talk to him about the necessity for periods of aridity and darkness, or of learning to face and live with certain experiences of darkness and accidie as they come, so I said to him: 'Well J, let me tell you what I did the other day. I climbed up Batcombe Ridge

140

above the friary, and from the top could see right over Dorset into Somerset – it was a fine day and even Glastonbury Tor was visible. Then out of breath, I lay down on the grass and looked into the sky. When I got my breath back, I began to sing to the Lord and dance, and then I rolled all the way back down the ridge, and returned to the friary with great joy and thanksgiving in my heart.'

'What?' said J, ' – but I can't do that.' 'Why not?' I asked, 'there's no-one there but the Lord, nobody else will see you.' 'Oh, but I would be there,' he replied, and looked rather sheepish and apologetic. 'Ah, there's the problem', said I. 'Come on now, why aren't you happy to be yourself, even before yourself . . .?' Well, then began a good conversation about the acceptance and loving of oneself, and later, J went off to think about it all.

About a fortnight later, we were talking again, and he said: 'I've been up to Batcombe Ridge.' 'Oh, have you?' I asked with a grin. 'And did you sing and roll all the way down?'

'Well, I *jumped*,' he replied, with a twinkle of humour in his eye.

References

1 St Maximus the Confessor speaks of the world as the 'Game of God', and this theme is developed in a serious-playful essay by Thomas Merton entitled, 'The General Dance', in *Seeds of Contemplation* (Wheathampstead: Anthony Clarke), pp. 225–230.

2 Alan Watts, *Beyond Theology* (New York: Random House Inc), p. 29.

3 Heb. 11:35–38.

4 See Thomas Merton, *Raids On The Unspeakable* (New York: New Directions), pp. 45–49.

5 Monica Furlong, *The End of Our Exploring* (London: Hodder & Stoughton), p. 85.

6 Deut. 14:2; 1 Pet. 2:9; 4:4.

7 1 Sam. 6:14–16; Acts 2:13.

8 1 Cor. 4:10–13. See also 1 Cor. 1:18–31.

9 Mark 3:21; Acts 26:24.

10 John of Ruysbroeck, *Adornment of the Spiritual Marriage* (London: J. M. Dent), pp. 69f.

11 See Evelyn Underhill, *Jacapone Da Todi* (London: J. M. Dent), pp. 76–80, and especially Laude LXXVI and LXXXIV).

9: Advice and Warning

This chapter is a ragbag of counsel and warning for would-be retreatants. Some of it is down to earth commonsense, and some of it concerns situations or dimensions which will be encountered on retreat. Some of the advice is humorous and some deadly serious; some of it is for everyone, and some for particularly sensitive souls, but it's all of use. So here goes:

Place and Cost
It seems counterproductive, in commending retreats, to sound a warning, but it is necessary here to make some practical coments which may not apply to all readers, and may not be relevant to many monastic venues. I refer to the practical matters of *where* to go and *how much* to pay. All this is relative, but retreats are becoming increasingly popular on the evangelical and catholic fronts (not to speak of other faiths and secular institutions), and the tradition of Franciscan simplicity causes me to question the need for both the luxury and the cost of some advertised venues.

Most monastic houses of all Orders give better fare and accommodation to their guests than they enjoy themselves, and this is only right. And many monastic houses do not make any definite charge, though they may give a basic guideline which is not obligatory. This means that no-one who is genuinely in need of retreat and cannot afford to pay is prohibited (though this is not a hint of free accommodation). But as I look through the new 'guidance literature' for retreat centres and come to know some of the costs involved, I am more and more convinced that it is not our Lord's will for us to spend excessive amounts of money for a period of cosseted life-style and expensive foods in a refurbished mansion in the country with pious people who know little of the world's poverty and pain. This is just a word of warning because subtle changes are taking place because of the commercial viability and attractiveness of making a retreat.

A good rule of thumb is to stick to the established Orders, and find out from friends and local parish priest/minister first. Is holiness such an expensive commodity? Well yes, it demands the whole of your life and talents – but it is for the poor as well as the rich, for the unemployed as well as the salaried. Our Lord ministered to rich and poor. And in any case, it is much better to live in simplicity or even a certain austerity in retreat, as long as the place affords basic accommodation and food, while guarding the silence and prayer.

Having sounded that warning note, it is usually the case that monastic and retreat accommodation is a lot less expensive than guesthouse/hotel costs, and speaking from our own experience, the cost in terms of money, work, time and talents is borne by the community brothers and sisters – but that is part of the joyful work that God has called us to do. And as St Benedict reminds us, we are to treat the guest as the Christ. And as St Paul puts it: 'Do not neglect to show hospitality to strangers, for thereby some have entertained angels unawares.'[1]

Take It Easy

The next piece of advice, especially to a new retreatant, is plain and simple – *Take it easy*! Some of the terms we use for people in need of this advice are very descriptive – they are 'buttoned-up' or 'up-tight'. Strain and tension exude from such people, and they are often frenetic in their activity and restless in their out of work hours. Not only so, but they produce tension and dis-ease all around them, giving out bad vibrations in company. In some cases, such tension and stress are symptoms of an underlying problem, and the cure is not to mask the symptoms by work, drink, drugs or escapist religion. Of course, it's no use telling a neurotic, depressed or up-tight person to 'snap out of it' on the one hand, or to 'take it easy' on the other. If the problem has a basic psychological cause, then that must be treated both spiritually and psychologically. And the making of a retreat may be the last thing such a person should contemplate, for exposure to solitude and silence may be dangerous for such a person. I am talking now about the ordinary anxious or up-tight person, the one for whom a week of retreat would be an oasis in the midst of a busy and frenetic world. That psychiatrist, coming on retreat to Glasshampton recently, said somewhat humorously: 'Lord deliver us from the human race.' I knew what he meant!

Take it easy, then, is the advice to be given to one who is tempted to fill the allotted time with stimulating reading, excessive exercise, exhausting manual work or relationship confrontations with other retreatants. It is a wonderful, a liberating experience just to do nothing. 'Sometimes I sits and thinks', runs a card motto on one of our friary walls, 'and sometimes I just sits!' I led a house group meeting during a mission just before my second period of six months' solitude, when two Hindu students were present. 'What are you going to do during your long period of solitude?' asked one of them. 'Nothing,' I replied, 'just nothing.' He grinned with sheer delight. 'Oh, that's the right answer,' he cried, and he knew that I was on the right track.

It is a very wonderful thing to be able to rest in the Lord physically and mentally, with the confidence of a child in its mother's arms, or to be able to learn how to do it by means of a simple discipline of prayer and meditation. One of the most beautiful and practical meditations from the Chinese tradition of *Chuang Tzu*, translated by Thomas Merton, communicates this gift-like ability to let go, and take it easy. It is a resolution of the discipline-spontaneity paradox, and is called: *When the Shoe Fits*:

> Ch'i the draftsman
> Could draw more perfect circles freehand
> Than with a compass.
>
> His fingers brought forth
> Spontaneous forms from nowhere. His mind
> Was meanwhile free and without concern
> With what he was doing.
> No application was needed

His mind was perfectly simple
And knew no obstacle.

So, when the shoe fits
The foot is forgotten,
When the belt fits
The belly is forgotten,
When the heart is right
'For' and 'against' are forgotten.

No drives, no compulsions,
No needs, no attractions:
Then your affairs
Are under control
You are a free man.

Easy is right. Begin right
And you are easy.
Continue easy and you are right.
The right way to go easy
Is to forget the right way
And forget that the going is easy.

Avoid Excessive Expectations

'Blessed is he who expects nothing', says a Charlie Brown
cartoon, 'for he shall not be disappointed.' That's sad as
well as funny, but there is basic common sense there. It is
counterproductive to go on retreat with a list of expectations, experiences, visions, locutions and spiritual high-
jumps demanded of the Lord. I often meet people who are
worried and anxious about the will of God for their lives.
They are always demanding, seeking, expecting and
imposing their expectations upon God. And he will have
none of it. If the Lord does not intend to make his way
known just now, there is no way in which we can resort to
magic, cajoling, pleading or demanding that will cause him
to conform to our expectations. This is certainly the case
in making a retreat. 'Rest in the Lord, wait patiently for
him,' says the psalmist, 'and he will give you the desires
of your heart.'

A day or week in retreat, like the will of God in one's
life, is a gradual unfolding. Of course there are exceptional

experiences when God suddenly apprehends a person when he least expects it, as when a lover creeps up upon his beloved and suddenly draws her close. But this does not happen outside a loving, trusting context. If you are wanting to know if the Lord wants you to rush into missionary service, to marry, to change your job, your country, your life-style, you must not expect to receive incontrovertible direction on demand, or even during the course of a retreat. Stop nagging and harassing the Lord. Allow him to speak, to guide, to lead at his own pace, in his own way, and according to his own rhythm. There is teaching about persistent, constant and availing prayer, but that only comes as a result of a deep knowledge of the ways of God. The story of Elijah praying for drought, and then for rain, is the story of a man led by the Spirit who, hearing the word and will of God, set about waiting upon him with anointed expectation. Then it could be said: 'The effectual, fervent prayer of a righteous man avails much.'[2] There was certainly compassion in the heart of Abraham, but all his bargaining with, and harassing of, God did not do any good.[3] God is the only ground and basis of our beseeching, and we must pray according to his will, allowing him to reveal that will and the method of its accomplishment. If we could believe and practise this, it would remove much of the strain and stress from our lives.

The basic purpose of a retreat is to let God have his way. It is for him to send sunshine or rain, pleasure or pain, darkness or light, appointment or disappointment, excitement or boredom. It is in times when one feels that nothing is being vouchsafed or accomplished that the deepest and most enduring interior work is done, and it is when we are endeavouring to organize and manipulate God that we experience frustration and impatience.

Practise a Gentle Discipline

We have been saying: 'Take it easy on yourself', and encouraging trust, rest, and a letting-go of anxieties, worries and manipulative expectations. But that is not to fall into laxity, sloth or downright laziness. There may be times when much of one's retreat is spent in sleep or in a horizontal posture of rest, but do not allow freedom from wordly demands to be the excuse for neglecting necessary disciplines. One cannot be spontaneous without a discipline, as one cannot be disciplined without a certain spontaneity. There is a middle way, and the advice given here is just to make one aware of the situation, and living experience and recourse to a friend or Spiritual Director will do the rest. Without being frenetic or destructively anxious, one can make the retreat a positive pilgrimage. From setting out from home, to the return following the retreat, there can be an exercise of gentle discipline in which there is an appropriate mix of the ingredients of spontaneity and mild asceticism.

The disciplines involved should be worked out beforehand with one's Director or Soul Friend, but will involve the liturgical framework of daily worship, time spent on manual and mental work, regulations about fasting, diet, exercise, reading and silence. If there is an imposed framework in which the retreat is set, there are fewer problems of organization, though the practice may be demanding. But if there is little or no framework, then time spent alone or with another in planning ahead becomes essential.

Two Possible Timetables

Presuming a week's retreat from Saturday to Saturday, an organized retreat may have a daily time schedule which looks like this:

6.30 a.m.	Rise and Ablutions
7.30 a.m.	Morning Prayer and Eucharist in Chapel
8.30 a.m.	Breakfast in Refectory with retreatants
9.00 a.m.	Spiritual reading or preparation for session
10.00 a.m.	Session 1: Talk/Input by Retreat Conductor
11.00 a.m.	Coffee break
11.30 a.m.	Either group work or workshop creative session (spiritual journal, calligraphy, painting, dream analysis, personal study)
12.45 p.m.	Midday Prayer in Chapel
1.00 p.m.	Lunch
	Afternoon free for Emmaus Walk in twos, or private walk
5.00 p.m.	Light tea

6.00 p.m.	Evening Prayer in Chapel
7.00 p.m.	Supper
8.00 p.m.	Group Meditation, or
	Session on the Jesus Prayer, leading into corporate silence
9.30 p.m.	Compline, and silence until morning

In a personal or silent retreat one may either fit oneself into the rhythm of the place (it may have silent meals and monastic offices), or attend a daily Eucharist and remain alone for the rest of the time along these lines:

6.30 a.m.	Rise, ablutions
7.30 a.m.	Eucharist in Chapel
8.30 a.m.	Breakfast
9.00 a.m.	Prayer and meditation exercise
10.00 a.m.	Reading and Study
11.00 a.m.	Coffee/Fruit Juice
11.30 a.m.	Artistic craft (spiritual journal etc as above)
12.45 p.m.	Reflection or Midday Office
1.00 p.m.	Preparation and taking of lunch
2.30 p.m.	Walking, jogging, swimming, practising 'mindfulness', manual work
5.00 p.m.	Light tea
6.00 p.m.	Prayer and meditation exercise
7.00 p.m.	Preparation and taking of supper
8.00 p.m.	Bread making etc./food preparation for morrow
9.00 p.m.	Spiritual reading, Compline, Reflection on day preceded or followed by short walk
10.00 p.m.	Retire

The latter time-table for an individual retreat may be changed according to circumstances. If the main meal is lunch, then of course jogging/swimming would not be advisable as the next item. I sometimes felt, during my long solitude, that I was being drawn away to meditation and prayer in the middle of manual work, and I would just drop what I was doing and enter into the trysting-place of prayer.

Psychological Darkness: Discernment and Insight

I have already indicated that there may be dangers in certain persons being exposed, without experience, to silence and solitude. Quite apart from those who suffer from forms of depression and anxiety symptoms, sudden and complete exposure to silence and solitude may produce negative psychological symptoms in otherwise ordinary, coping people.

Part of the novice training within the Society of St Francis is the eight months each novice must spend at our house of prayer at Glasshampton. Some look forward immensely to this time, and others view its approach with increasing apprehension. It often turns out to be the opposite of their expectations on both counts! It means that novices are moved often from busy, active, social and challenging surroundings, where their ministry is needed, appreciated and rewarded, to an enclosure and a certain quietness where all the hidden or repressed questions which may have been tucked away in the recesses of the psyche come to the surface. The challenges and fears of poverty, celibacy and obedience come to the fore. Confrontation with questions of aloneness, sexuality, stability and human relations has priority on the agenda. The question: 'What am I doing here?' which involves these and other matters, soon becomes the question of identity: 'Who am I?' And this is where the real pilgrimage begins, for it is as possible to evade the fundamental questions of existence and identity by taking cover in a pseudo-religion as it is by running to drink, drugs, sex or the bright lights of entertainment, money or power. When religion becomes an opiate instead of a challenge to the depths of one's creativity, potentiality and identity, then things have gone terribly wrong. Bad religion gives birth to dogmatism, callousness, exclusiveness and hard judgmental attitudes.

Within our Order there are pastoral and counselling structures which make one aware of this situation, and provide for the care and instruction necessary for the working through of one's own psychological and spiritual journey. There is a clear recognition of the dangers of such exposure to enclosure and solitude, and the availability of spiritual and psychological direction and help so that novices and professed are able to continue their pilgrimage in hope and joy. Occasional retreatants need only be aware of this dimension and not try too much too soon. Advice and counsel is usually available.

Participating Guests
There are certain guests who come to Glasshampton annually, and their joy and discipline is in the sharing of our silence, solitude and worship, for in such a house of prayer, there is a non-verbal sharing of life, worship, meals and work. A parish priest who comes regularly to us has a wise wife, and she recently sent him for an extended retreat because he needed not only the atmosphere of prayer and silence for the good of his own soul, but also the context in which to think and work out his future ministry, bearing in mind the awareness of God's will and the needs of his family who are all involved. Because he is an experienced priest and man of prayer, he received direction in the form of a weekly sharing of thought and prayer with one of the friars. The outcome was an interior renewal to which he bore witness in joy and tears, and which is being spelled out in greater fruitfulness in his ministry. I took our novices to his multi-racial parish last week where we were involved in meeting Hindus, Buddhists, Jews and Sikhs, all of whom live in the midst of increasingly threatening secularization and violence.

In chapter five a young man from the east end of London writes of his week alone in the prayer-hut in our garden enclosure. On the last day of his retreat he shared with me some of the fruits of his silence and prayer. It was obvious that he was very aware of the joys, challenges and dangers of such a time of seclusion. He entered creatively into the week, becoming aware that his life of prayer and meditation was taken up not only into the beauty and harmony of the world of nature by which he was surrounded, but also by the sorrows and pains of a perplexed and perplexing world in which famine, drought, violence, tyranny and nuclear accident had been manifested that very week. The best way he knew of nourishing his spiritual roots and renewing his physical and spiritual life was to enter into an experience of retreat in the context of a monastery.

The Dark Night: Redemption and Contemplation

I have elsewhere written of the dark night in which the believer is involved in the pursuit of a deeper life of prayer.[4] The pattern of patriarchs, apostles and of our Lord himself is a clear representation and warning of those dark powers, both psychological and spiritual, which are unleashed when we allow ourselves to be taken deeper into the life of prayer. As soon as we practise the simple methods of prayerful awareness of the presence of God by right posture, correct breathing and invocation of the name of Jesus, then we begin to live at deeper depths than we have known previously. And when we allow those depths of our interior life to surface, it is not always a wholesome experience at first, for we are a *microcosm*, a little world. We become caught up in the sins, evasions and selfish complexities of our age and world, and become intensely aware of the interior violence, sin and darkness which is the sad inheritance of an alienated humanity.

This is the reason why penitence, confession and forgiveness are at the beginning of the life of prayer. Whenever the patriarch, prophet or apostle is exposed to the blinding holiness of God's love, there is a cry of searing pain and longing, an awareness of one's sin, the need for repentance, forgiveness and healing, and the intense longing for a new life and the contemplative vision of God. This is the pattern of scripture, the way of the mystics and the path of every believer who is in earnest with God.

Progressive Sanctification

There is a pattern, a plan, a path, a pilgrimage, and it is well to know the map of the terrain before one makes the terrible journey. The map is not the journey, neither is the description the experience. Many people read the Bible, or the story of the great pilgrims of prayer, and *imagine* they have taken the path themselves because they have read about it. It is necessary, with the Spirit in one's heart, the Bible in one's hand, and one's feet planted firmly within the fellowship of the pilgrim Church, to actually *make* the journey. Without the map there is no awareness of either the pitfalls or the shining vistas of glory, but it is not enough to study the map or learn it by heart – the journey must be made.

I use the term *Progressive Sanctification* because it indicates dynamic movement and perpetual cleansing and awareness. From the moment that the sinner is graced with a vision of the crucified, risen and glorified Christ, there is effected by the interior operation of the Holy Spirit, a psychic and spiritual transformation that takes one into ever higher degrees of glory.[5] It may begin with an evangelical conversion, or at least with a deepening realization of one's unlikeness to God, and a turning from sin to receive God's full and free forgiveness. But this is only the beginning. From that moment the real *purgation* begins, a purging of the dross, a cleansing of the defilement, and a radical reorientation of one's life, from the self-centred ego to the renewal of the image of God. There is both pain and ecstasy involved in such an interior work of God, and there are times when the wrestling Jacob becomes an apt parable of the soul's relationship with God. There is conflict, struggle, despair and ecstasy experienced, but once the wrestling has been initiated by the mysterious God in the solitude and darkness of the soul's night, there is no letting go. The omnipotent God will not let go the agonizing soul, and the soul clings to the wrestling God, for its very life and salvation are in the balance, and the mystery of the soul's identity is at stake.

But following upon the work of purgation is the experience of *illumination*. When the risen Christ confronted Saul on the Damascus Road, he shone his light of love and holiness into the murky depths of Saul's heart, illuminating the darkest corner and searing him with all the glorious pain of discovery and interior love. 'Who are you, Lord?' cried out Saul. And this was the beginning of a life cleansed and illumined by the Spirit of God. Such is the power of spiritual illumination that the world of the spirit overflows in a transfiguring of the natural order. Not only do I see that the crucified Jesus is the Lord of Glory, but his cross becomes his throne and blossoms as the tree of life. Then men, women and children around me are filled with the compassion and love of God, and nature begins to sing:

Heaven above is softer blue,
Earth around is sweeter green;
Something lives in every hue
Christless eyes have never seen:
Birds with gladder songs o'erflow,
Flowers with deeper beauties shine,
Since I know as now I know,
I am his and he is mine.

It was many years before I could begin to read the writings of St John of the Cross, that prince of mystics. Even now, I am often stopped in my tracks as I am filled with wonder at the light and illumination that blazed into his dark cell of persecution, while his soul was exposed to the blazing glory of God's love. In speaking of this progressive sanctification, he likens the soul to a damp log, and the divine light of illumination is the fire. The process is one in which the log of damp wood is taken up into the warmth, light and heat of the flame. Firstly the fire begins to dry the log, expelling the moisture. This makes it black and unsightly, causing it to give out a bad smell. But the process continues and the purging gives way to kindling, to warmth and to heat, until by transformation, the fire takes hold upon the log and transfigures it into its own nature.[6]

So *purgation* and *illumination* give way to *union*. And this can begin in the present life for the lover of God. It does not satisfy the lover to be purged and freed from his blindness and disabilities, nor yet to be able to gaze upon the beauties of his beloved in the glory of illumination. He must press on to union – he must *know* her in the most profound meaning of that word, entering physically, psychically and spiritually into deepest union with his beloved, until there is a fusion of body and spirit in unutterable groaning and yearning, fulfilment and consummation. Both scripture and the mystical tradition of the Church use the analogy of sexual union to portray and symbolize the union of Christ and his Church, of Christ and the believer. The commentaries of St Bernard of Clairvaux, and supremely the poetry of St John of the Cross demonstrate such disciplined and refined usage. The discipline of steel and the outpourings of ecstasy are contained within the same stanzas. Here is the place where spontaneity and discipline come together in inspired outpouring, in an endeavour to describe the ineffable – the union of the soul with God. And it even becomes too much for him:

Of that breathing of God I should not wish to speak, neither do I desire now to speak; for I see clearly that I cannot say aught concerning it, and that, were I to speak of it, it would seem less than it is. For it is a breathing of God himself, wherein, in that awakening of lofty knowledge of the Deity, the Holy Spirit breathes into the soul in proportion to the knowledge wherein He most profoundly absorbs it in the Holy Spirit, inspiring it with most delicate love for Himself according to that which it has seen; for the soul, being full of blessing and glory, the Holy Spirit has filled it with goodness and glory, wherein He has inspired it with a love for Himself which transcends all description and all sense in the deep things of God. And for that reason I leave speaking of it here.[7]

At the outset of this chapter I commented that it would be a ragbag of counsel and warning, and this has ranged from basic, commonsense advice, to lofty theological counsels. Well, not to make heavy weather of the last paragraphs let me include two pieces of advice from that attractive Franciscan hermit, Ramon Lull, writing for hermit brothers in the thirteenth century. His lovable irony may indicate high motivation for retreat in solitude:

The Lover longed for solitude and he went away to live alone so that he might have the companionship of his Beloved, for he was lonely amongst many people.

The Lover was all alone in the shade of a fair tree. Men passed by that place and they asked him why he was alone. And the lover answered, 'I am alone now that I have seen you and heard you. Until now I was in the company of my Beloved.'[8]

References

1 Heb. 13:2.

2 See James 5:16–18; 1 Kings 17:1; 18:1, 41–46.

3 Gen. 18:22–33.

4 See *HF* pp. 177ff.

5 See 2 Cor 3:18; 4:6; Phil. 3:10–14.

6 St John of the Cross, *The Dark Night of the Soul*, Bk. II, X, 1.

7 ibid., *Living Flame of Love*, IV. 17.

8 *The Book of the Lover and the Beloved*, verses 41 and 47 (London: SPCK).

10: Prayer, Meditation, Contemplation

Diversity in Prayer

There are many forms of prayer, both personal and corporate, liturgical and extempore, and the Christian who explores the dimensions of prayer may think of such exploration as an adventure, a pilgrimage, a challenge and a duty. It is all of these things, and the varied forms of prayer are all open to the individuals and groups who wish to participate in them.

Since our theme is retreats, we are concerned with liturgical and free prayer, and with corporate sharing and personal exploration. Corporate and liturgical prayer is already provided in a retreat or monastic house, and the retreatant may respond as he sees fit to what is offered. Therefore I am not concerned with the liturgical usage of any particular monastic house in this book, but with the 'extra-liturgical' levels of prayer that draw us into a deeper awareness of God's loving presence, with the ability to enter into meditation through scripture or thematic approaches to the creativity of God in the world. Also there is the whole area of contemplative prayer in which one is held within the silence and adoration of God into which we shall be increasingly drawn if we are faithful to the disciplines of prayer.

Again, I do not intend to deal directly with verbal prayers of adoration, thanksgiving, petition, complaint or intercession because presumably these are part of one's ordinary diet of teaching at local Church and prayer-group level. My concern here is with those areas which will allow experiment and evolving experience as time and concentration is given to disciplines which are clearly part of the ancient tradition, but which have been neglected in parish teaching.

Meditation and the Body

It is becoming more obvious that the body must be taken up into prayer. We do not pray with our brains – it is not a merely intellectual exercise. This is not to say that our prayers are unplanned or irrational, but when we have moved out of public forms of liturgy or intercession, and into personal meditative and contemplative prayer we are allowing ourselves to be instruments of prayer. We can then become the flute through which the inspiration and expiration of the Holy Spirit of God constantly breathes. This is exactly what St Paul indicates:

> Likewise the Spirit helps us in our weakness; for we do not know how to pray as we ought, but the Spirit himself intercedes for us with sighs too deep for words (lit. groanings inexpressible). And he who searches the hearts of men knows what is the mind of the Spirit, because the Spirit intercedes for the saints according to the will of God.[1]

The fulness of trinitarian movement is at work in meditative and contemplative prayer, for it is the Father who is in all, through all and above all who calls us to participation in his divine life. It is through the cosmic, mediating work of Christ, the eternal Logos, that we are brought into saving and reconciling relationship with the Father, and it is by the indwelling Spirit that we are profoundly moved from within the depths of our hearts to cry out in love and adoration. Such prayer involves the fulness of our being, for again St Paul's holistic vision of prayer embraces spirit, soul and body. The body is the temple of the Holy Spirit, and we are enjoined to present our body to the Lord in worship and adoration.[2]

The Holy Spirit is thought of as the breath of God in scripture, and it is a profitable exercise to trace this analogy throughout the Bible and in hymnology, discovering the heartbeat and respiration of God not only in the manifestation of rhythmic life in the created order, but also in the reconciling and redeeming movement of God in the ministry of Christ and the sanctifying work of the Spirit.

It is not so much that we engage in prayer, but that we

are caught up into the divine movement of prayer, into an experiential participation in the trinitarian life of God – we are being 'prayed through' as it were. Our spirit, soul and body are drawn into the creative movement of love, so that we are made vehicles or instruments of the Holy Spirit. If this is what prayer is about, we shall experience the dynamic and sanctifying power of the Spirit in every part of our being, and the overflow of the divine life and love will manifest itself in compassion and creativity in the world. We may think of Jesus as the eternal Word dwelling within the bosom of the Father, or as being enveloped and transfigured in the uncreated energies of God upon the holy mountain, but as we see him practically engaged in his ministry in the gospels, we observe the outcome, the consequence, the overflow of this contemplative dimension:

> God anointed Jesus of Nazareth with the Holy Spirit and with power. . . . He went about doing good and healing all that were oppressed by the devil, for God was with him.[3]

Prayer as Gift and Discipline

There is a sheer gift-like quality about true prayer – it is a charism, an anointing of the Holy Spirit. 'You have no need that anyone should teach you', says St John, 'because you have an anointing from the Holy One.'[4] This is a basic insight, a fundamental experience concerning prayer. It means that, at times, the Holy Spirit will so move the believer, or the corporate worshipping group, that there will be an inspired response, an anointed awakening, a profound movement of love, in which it is obvious and clear that the Holy Spirit is in control. This may manifest itself in liturgical beauty, in charismatic gifts, in personal or corporate silence, but it will certainly result in life-giving adoration or perhaps burdened intercession.

Again, it will take up the wholeness of one's body, mind and spirit, and the experience recorded in scripture and in mystical writings uses language like being filled, possessed, baptized, caught up, anointed, moved, inspired, entranced or slain by the Holy Spirit. Experiences like this may happen after a long period of waiting, seeking and yearning.

159

Or they may be completely spontaneous, and will take hold of the believer or group without warning, without apparent preparation, as the lover steals up to his beloved and surprises her with the enveloping power of his tenderness and love.

Experiences like this are to be valued and expected in the life of prayer, but they are only part of the story. Prayer, as well as being a gift, is a discipline, and requires time and effort, fasting and preparation. This may continue in burden and vigil through nights and days of aridity and darkness. Faithfulness in the discipline of prayer is the complement to the inspired and spontaneous charisms that visit us in sheer, generous grace.

If you have learned to ride a bicycle, to swim, roller skate, drive a car or play an instrument, it is clear that there are times when you trust yourself to the balance of the cycle, the buoyancy of the water, but also many hours, months, years of continual application and practice on the keyboard or flute, until proficiency is achieved and becomes second nature. The result is a gift and a discipline – to the onlooker it looks so easy! The ease and proficiency which are the result, belie the long hours of disciplined application, but nevertheless become a joyful reward.

One of our postulants was an organist of some ability. I remember well the walk we shared one day as we talked about prayer and discipline, while he described to me the discipline and inspiration that he experienced in his involvement with music. 'I take up one of Bach's Prelude and Fugue studies,' he said, 'one which I want so much to learn. First of all I look through it, evaluate it, try to get a little of the feel and sense of the composer. Then I take it to the organ and begin the long discipline of application and learning. I have to use my eyes, my ears, my hands, my feet, and try to co-ordinate all together in the making of the music – this music. As time goes on and I get the feel of the music and the mind of the composer, there comes a time when things begin to flow. Then co-ordination happens and my eyes and ears and hands and feet co-operate with mind and heart, and I get taken up into the music, and the music begins to play itself through me – something has happened and I am part of it all.'

I have not reported his words verbatim, but this is the substance of what he said, and as I listened, I felt the joy and spontaneity of the discipline and charism of prayer flow through me. For he seemed to me to be talking about life in the Spirit, or the way of prayer. After periods of darkness and vigil, of waiting and longing, of application and groaning, there comes a time when the Spirit himself pours into the heart the stirrings of the divine love, and then the Spirit prays himself through the believer in groaning and sighing, in longing and adoration, in beseeching and crying . . . and ultimately in the wonder of silence and possession. And when this happens, it is worth all the work and discipline, for the sorrow is turned into joy. 'When a woman is in travail she has sorrow because her hour has come; but when she is delivered of the child, she no longer remembers the anguish, for joy that a child is born into the world.'[5]

Practical Application

It is one thing to affirm that the life of prayer should call into play all our powers of mind and body, but quite another to live a life where this is our everyday experience. It goes without saying that we can use eyes, ears, tongue, hands and feet, mind and heart in the worship of God. It is also obvious that prayer is not confined to any one posture. One can pray standing, sitting, walking, dancing, kneeling or prostrate. But many of our postures in daily life are not conducive to stillness and silence. We are frenetic, restless, full of nervous tension and unchannelled energies. If we cannot sit still in the patient tranquillity of love and prayer then it is obvious that our minds are not at peace, and that we are possessed of restlessness of spirit.

Of course, stillness of body is not prayer, it is but a form of preparation. It is no good teaching methods or techniques of bodily relaxation and stillness if one's heart is full of unresolved anger and hatred, or if one's mind is distracted and fragmented by broken relationships. Repentance, forgiveness and reconciliation are prerequisites of prayer. As Jesus said: 'If you are offering your gift at the altar, and there remember that your brother has something against you, leave your gift there before the altar and go;

first be reconciled to your brother, and then come and offer your gift.'[6] It is only a man who has experienced forgiveness and reconciliation and who seeks to live in peace with all men who is truly able to pray. This matter of conversion of one's life is primary, and if that is right, then we can proceed with the teaching.

Inward Stillness: Posture and Breathing

Interior stillness is the basic attitude, which includes stillness of body. This means selecting a good posture. Find a room, a hut, a chapel or the open air. It doesn't matter where, as long as there are no distractions. Wear loose clothing (a track suit is fine), no footwear, then sit on a chair or stool, a prayer stool or a cushion. You may lie on your back or tummy if you want, or adopt the semi-lotus, lotus or perfect postures. It doesn't matter as long as it is without strain or discomfort. Keep your back straight.

Now in your chosen posture, begin from the soles of your feet and enumerate the parts of your body, stretching and relaxing them as you enumerate until you achieve a physical rest and stillness. There's no strain or anxiety about this, everything must be easy and slow and gentle – it's not competitive, but passive and restful. If you've never done this before, it may be best the first time to learn this simple relaxation technique lying on your back with the palms of your hands upward at your side. But whatever your posture, do it now:

My whole body is being given over to passivity and rest. I submit myself to the healing peace and love of God as I let go . . . let go . . . and rest in him.
I enumerate the parts of my body, stretching and relaxing as I do . . . the soles of my feet . . . my ankles . . . calves . . . thighs . . . buttocks . . . abdomen . . . back . . . chest . . . hands . . . arms . . . shoulders . . . neck . . . throat . . . face . . . head . . . gently . . . letting go . . . relaxing . . . gently . . . trustingly . . . in the Father's love.

Breath of God

Already, if you have brought your body co-operatively into a state of relaxed rest, you will have found that your breathing is slower and deeper. This is the effect of allowing tension and strain to drain away. A person who is frightened, anxious, frenetic, breathes quickly, with shallow, gasping breaths, from the upper chest. Gentle, slow, deep breathing from the diaphragm is what you need. It is both the product of a relaxed calm, and produces a calming effect. This is belly-breathing as opposed to shallow chest breathing. Now let's practise:

First of all, *note* your breathing. Now slowly control the rate of breathing, gently deepen it, with slower, deeper breaths, making it rhythmic and regular. No strain, no anxiety, but gentle, slow, deep, regular, rythmic breaths, settling into a new, gentle pattern, your pattern, an easy pattern. Continue with this for some minutes, in the continuing state of rest and gentleness.

When the rhythm is established and easy, try this simple exercise. Count 'one-two' on the inspiration, 'one-two' on the pause, and 'one-two-three-four' on the expiration. You may find it a little difficult at first, but persevere gently, and it will establish itself, at its own rate:

In / Pause / Out
1–2 / 1–2 / 1–2–3–4

Continue with this for a few minutes, being aware of the incoming and outgoing breath, remembering that the air that you breathe is filled with the presence and power of God. The Spirit of God is within, without and all around you, enveloping you in the loving embrace of God . . .

If the exercise helps, continue with it. If not, then fall back upon your own quiet, deep, gentle, belly-breathing at your own rate. Let yourself be carried down and more deeply into yourself through breathing. It is natural and gentle. There is nothing to fear, for it is all within the gentle love of God your creator, and the Spirit of God is within you.

At this point, many people find that they begin to repeat the *Jesus Prayer* with their lips, then in their minds, eventually allowing it to sink into their hearts: 'Lord Jesus Christ,

Son of God, have mercy on me, a sinner.'[7] Other people now begin their meditation upon scripture or a given theme. If you are following a pattern of scripture meditation, then this is the kind of preparation you may follow, going on with the reading of the scripture, while maintaining a quiet and meditative spirit.

Heartbeat

Preparation for meditation or contemplative prayer varies for different temperaments. I find that when I have relaxed into the kind of gentle, rhythmic breathing described above, I then become aware of my heartbeat, without having to feel for it at my radial pulse. I follow it, and bring my breathing into co-ordination with it, and after some time, I either rest in God for the whole of the meditation period, or begin the Jesus Prayer within the rhythm of my heartbeat. Psychosomatically, this linking of body rhythm with the repetition of the Jesus Prayer is a primary spiritual way for me. Of course, this is only possible when praying alone. The Jesus Prayer said corporately must go at the rhythm of the leader, but such a surrender of the personal to the corporate rhythm is itself both a discipline and a joy.

The importance of the heartbeat rhythm in contemplative prayer or in a prayer of repetition like the Jesus Prayer is that there is a cosmic dimension to it. My own pulse echoes the cosmic pulse, and by and through it I am related to the created order as a creature, and to the Holy Spirit as the Lord, the life-giver. The Holy Spirit who moved and brooded over the face of the waters at creation, and is the principle of creative harmony and order in the cosmos, is the Spirit who wrought the incarnation of the divine Logos in the womb of Mary, and thereby brought about redemption. This same Spirit of creation and redemption dwells in the most interior cave of my heart, and in contemplative prayer I savour his indwelling, and through him, communion with the Father and the Son.

In an hour of prayer, a quiet day, or a week or more of

retreat, the above method is one which brings me into the area of meditative and contemplative prayer, and is the basic norm for stillness before and in God.

References

1 Romans 8:26, 27.
2 1 Thess. 5:23; 1 Cor. 3:16; Rom. 12:1.
3 Acts 10:38.
4 1 John 2:21.
5 John 16:21.
6 Matt. 5:23, 24.
7 See 'The Jesus Prayer', in *HF* pp. 118ff.

11: Using the Bible in Retreat

In any monastic or conducted retreat, the Bible will have pride of place. Retreat is a context in which the Bible is the basic teaching source. It not only includes the fundamental, primordial revelation of God in the Judaistic and Christian traditions, but serves also as a book of worship, ethics and inspiration, corporate and personal, for the people of God. I shall summarize the uses of scripture in the context of retreat, and then spend a little more time on the meditative use of the Bible in times of prayer.

The Bible as Liturgy

Unless you spend time in complete or near solitude, you will probably join in the monastic daily round of worship, or at least with your own retreat group. This may include the saying/singing of offices (Morning, Midday, Evening Prayer and Compline), and the daily celebration of the Eucharist.

The word *liturgy* means *service* in the sense that it is an offering to God of worship, ministry and adoration.[1] When the Church offers liturgy in this sense it presents the gift and work of adoration, praise and prayer through Christ by the power of the Spirit as a worthy offering to the Father. This is a basic part of Christian service. In such liturgy there is the reading and hearing of Old and New Testament scripture, the repeating/chanting of psalms and canticles from all parts of the canon of scripture. At the Eucharist there may be an Old Testament reading, and an epistle and gospel reading. The eucharistic prayer is a beautiful weaving of gospel teaching into a biblical fabric of offering, thanksgiving and sacrifice. Liturgy in a monastic house is the saturation of the life of worship with scripture as primary, for the sacramental life flows from its source in scripture.

The Bible as Teaching

In a remarkably succinct paragraph,[2] William Barclay expounds four New Testament Greek words which denote the early Christian preaching, and they all have to do with the communication of the Gospel in scripture, presenting different facets of biblical truth.

The first word is *kergyma*, which may be rendered *proclamation*. It is a herald's announcement of the Faith which is most surely believed, proclaimed with confidence – a plain, uncompromising announcement of Christian truth. Then there is *didache*, which means *teaching*. This expounds the *kergyma*, and is the didactic unfolding of the implications of the fundamental truths. Then there is *paraklesis*, which means *exhortation*, and is the appeal to the hearers to take heed, believe, and act upon what they have heard. And lastly, *homilia* is the *discoursing-treatment* of a subject in the light of Christian truth.

All these words may be operative in a teaching retreat, for it is impossible to separate these strands. The saving Gospel is proclaimed, expounded, exhorted and applied, and the truths of the *kerygma* are clarified for our belief and action within the context of the other three words.

The Immediacy of Scripture

Of course, there are many levels at which the reading, hearing and preaching of scripture affects the one attending to it. It can be startling, immediately powerful, searing or cutting: 'The word of God is living and active, sharper than any two-edged sword, piercing to the division of soul and spirit, of joints and marrow, and discerning the thoughts and intentions of the heart.'[3]

In the third century in Egypt, Antony was a rich young man who heard the gospel words: 'If you would be perfect, go, sell what you have and give it to the poor and come, follow Me.' He was stunned, capitulated, and became the father of Christian eremitic (hermit) life. Nearly a century later, Augustine, under conviction of sin, recalled the story of Antony, and near to tears, sitting in a garden in Milan, he suddenly heard a child's voice chanting: '*Tolle lege, Tolle lege*' – 'take and read, take and read'. So he took up the New Testament, let it fall open, and read: 'Let us conduct ourselves becomingly, as in the day, not in revelling and drunkenness, not in debauchery and licentiousness, not in quarrelling and jealousy. But put on the Lord Jesus Christ, and make no provision for the flesh, to gratify its desires.' Response was immediate:

I had no wish to read more and no need to do so. For in an instant, as I came to the end of the sentence, it was as though the light of confidence flooded into my heart and all the darkness of doubt was dispelled.[4]

In the thirteenth century, Francis of Assisi was apprehended by the power of scripture. If you visit Assisi, just a few kilometres below the town is the still existing tiny Portiuncula Chapel, then lost in the woods, but now enclosed in the immense Basilica of *Santa Maria degli Angeli* – all rather ironic in the context of Francis' love of poverty. Here it was that Francis heard the reading of the Gospel for the day:

These twelve Jesus sent out, charging them, 'The kingdom of heaven is at hand. Heal the sick, raise the dead, cleanse lepers, cast out demons. You received without pay, give without pay. Take no gold, nor silver, nor copper in your belts, no bag for your journey, nor two tunics, nor sandals, nor a staff; for the labourer deserves his food. . . . As you enter a house salute it. And if the house is worthy, let your peace come upon it . . .'[5]

He asked the priest to explain its meaning, and Francis trembled with happiness at such a revelation and cried out with enthusiasm: 'This is what I wish, this is what I am seeking, this I long with all my inmost heart to do.' And off he went, and soon many thousands of Franciscan friars were living such a gospel life.

It was on 24th May, 1783, that John Wesley had such an experience. He had opened his Greek New Testament at 5.00 a.m. and read: 'There are given unto us exceeding great and precious promises, even that ye should be partakers of the divine nature.' And opening it again he read: 'Thou art not far from the kingdom of God.' In the afternoon he went to Evensong at St Paul's Cathedral, and the anthem was Psalm 130, *De Profundis*, which Wesley quotes from the Book of Common Prayer. In the evening he went unwillingly to a society in Aldersgate Street where he heard read Luther's Preface to the Epistle to the Romans. He records in his diary:

> About a quarter before nine, while he was describing the change which God works in the heart through faith in Christ, I felt my heart strangely warmed. I felt I did trust in Christ, Christ alone for salvation; and an assurance was given me that he had taken away *my* sins, even *mine*, and saved *me* from the law of sin and death.[6]

The immediacy of the inspired word, the inward longing and response, the enthusiasm and the burning heart – they are all part of the powerful experience of hearing the saving word of God in scripture. And this is all reminiscent of the Emmaus story, when two disciples walked in perplexity and loneliness after the death of Jesus. When he drew near and walked with them, he questioned them, diagnosed their condition, and led them to himself in scripture: 'And beginning with Moses and all the prophets, he interpreted to them in all the scriptures the things concerning himself.' The effect of this was that having reached the village, and asking him to bless and break the bread, their eyes were suddenly opened and they recognized him, as scripture and personal presence ran together in an immediacy of experience that caused them to say to one another: 'Did not our heart burn within us while he talked with us on the road, while he opened to us the scriptures.'

In their enthusiasm, they rushed back the seven or so miles to Jerusalem and burst in on the disciples, but they were already in a ferment because the news had broken. Then suddenly Jesus stood among them, and after beautiful words of calm and faith, he showed them his hands and feet, ate a piece of broiled fish in his transfigured body, and Luke records:

Then he said to them, 'These are my words which I

spoke to you while I was still with you, that everything written about me in the law of Moses and the prophets and the psalms must be fulfilled.' Then he opened their minds to understand the scriptures.[7]

Scripture and Meditation

Scripture is recited and shared liturgically, and is preached and expounded in retreat addresses, but it must not stop there. It must become the fuel and food of contemplative meditation.

It is clear that there must be open eyes, an open mind and an open heart. This indicates the dimensions of the physical, the mental and the spiritual. Meditation on scripture is not teaching or bible study, and though you may have a devotional commentary with you, it is naked exposure to scripture that must be involved, not second opinion upon the letter of scripture.

Perhaps the best analogy to use is that of a love letter. When a lover receives such a letter, he does not seek other people's opinions about it; he does not approach it in a coldly objective or academic manner; he does not analyze it as to etymological origins, grammatical structure or syntactical techniques. He is not interested in grammar and syntax at that moment, but in his beloved! He will savour the letter, read it slowly, carefully, tenderly. He will re-read it, not only the words it says, but its inner and hidden meanings, discoverable only to him. He will thrill to the feel of it, the smell, touch and texture of it – not because of the paper or odour or ink, but because of the touch and scent and presence of his beloved in it. He will feel, though others may not, the vibrations set up within himself by the letter, and he will understand, interpret, and even place it inside his shirt and near to his heart. All this is nonsense to the investigator who will carry out quite other examinations upon the letter, in terms of literary criticism, bringing to bear all the conceptual paraphernalia of critical method.

Understand! I am not decrying such objective investigation of the Bible – it has its time and place. But it is secondary. It is not the way of meditation, leading to contemplative prayer. Neither am I commending a fundamentalist approach which would lead to bibliolatry, for as

St Paul says: 'the written code kills, but the Spirit gives life.' The lover does not savour and treasure the letter for the letter's sake, but for the sake of the beloved it communicates. He does not fight over etymology or plenary inspiration, but the inspiration of the heart and spirit. The letter actually conveys and communicates the beloved in its own particular way.

The purpose of the letter, then, is to mediate the presence of the beloved. And meditation of scripture is also to that end. With this difference – the letter can only mediate, communicate, revitalize in the *absence* of the beloved. What purpose would the letter serve if the beloved was herself present? The beloved would lay aside the letter (precious though it still would be), and take the beloved in his arms. What madness and stupidity if he insisted on reading the letter to the beloved, commenting upon turns of phrase, beauty of structure, reciting its poetry and singing its praises. She could well say: 'What are you doing? Lay the letter aside, for I am here before you – delight in *me*, and take me to yourself, for I love you!'

Christ's Presence in Scripture

In the catholic tradition, Orthodox, Roman and Anglican, much is rightly made of the presence of Christ in the Eucharist.[8]

In such a tradition the sacrament is precious and the celebration of the Eucharist and the receiving of our Lord in Holy Communion is a vital part of revealed Faith. This is true of most other parts of the Church too (excepting the Quakers and the Salvation Army). But it is as necessary to speak of the real presence of Christ in scripture. When scripture is read, preached, expounded, truly and in the power of the Holy Spirit, then the real presence of Christ is mediated savingly to the hearers, and they are smitten, converted, healed, sustained, encouraged or condemned, – whatever the need may be. So in the meditative use of scripture, if the eyes, mind and heart have been opened and anointed, then Christ will enter in.

This begets an expectant attitude in the meditator. If you take any of the desert and retreat stories in the biblical background section of this book, or apply yourself to the seven days' retreat material at the end of the book, then this expectant attitude will bear fruit. Fr Kallistos Ware writes from the Orthodox tradition: 'As a book uniquely inspired by God and addressed to each of the faithful personally, the Bible possesses sacramental power, transmitting grace to the reader, bringing him to a point of meeting and decisive encounter.'[9]

This sanctified sense of anticipation and the use of dedicated imagination is needful so that one lives within scripture as if present, so that its truth becomes part of one's living experience. This is the promise that God gives:

> For as the rain and the snow come down from heaven, and return not thither but water the earth, making it bring forth and sprout, giving seed to the sower and bread to the eater, so shall my word be that goes forth from my mouth; it shall not return to me empty, but it shall accomplish that which I purpose and prosper in the thing for which I sent it.[10]

If you prepare yourself as outlined in the previous chapter, or as outlined in the introduction to the *Pattern for a Seven Day Retreat*, you will find yourself at the place where scripture is open before you, and you are open to God. Bearing in mind what has been said about the lover and the beloved above, be aware that God loves you unconditionally, fills you with his presence and longs to communicate himself to you. This will not always be evident in your emotional response – it may be a matter not of feeling but of faith and affirmation. The Lord does sometimes overwhelm one with a sense of his presence, or sometimes imparts a sense of quiet and interior rest and peace, but a particular emotional response may be merely incidental. Your part is to continue to follow gently and slowly the reading of scripture, savour the words, enter into its meaning, place yourself within the context of the passage, stay within the silence, and repeat words or sentences verbally or in your mind and heart. Writing about meditation on the gospels, Fr John Veltri gives five key words, summarizing this experience with Jesus in a gospel passage:

1) *Be There With Him* and for him, giving him mind and heart.
2) *Want Him*, hunger for him. Prepare for his coming and his word as you would the dearest person in your life. Invite him to reveal himself, his love to you, to speak to you and teach you how to listen to him.
3) *Listen to Him* with faith, deeply and reverently and trustfully. Forget about implications, application, conclusions, resolutions. Be simple, like a child nestled in its father's lap, peacefully listening to his story.
4) *Let Him.* Let him be with you . . . be for you what he wants to be. Let him love you . . . speak to you . . . hold you . . . console and strengthen you. Let him take you through dryness and darkness if that's what he wants, but let him. What Jesus wants, Jesus deserves. Trust yourself to him.
5) *Respond to Him* – in any way you feel moved to. Be genuinely yourself, responding honestly, freely, reverently, saying what is in your heart including complaining. Remember when you don't know what to say, the Holy Spirit prays in and for you. Just speaking or whispering the name of Jesus rhythmically with your breathing, or repeating words of adoration and praise are profoundly prayerful responses.

You will soon be able to do away with these simple methods, or just take them up occasionally at the beginning of your meditative prayer. It is all a matter of bringing yourself as you are, with all your glory and pain, into the healing and loving presence of God, so that he can transform you from without and within.

From Meditation to Contemplation

It is difficult to draw border lines in the way of prayer. These two words are meant to indicate the movement from the area where we are at work preparing, expecting, opening, longing, inviting, and resting in his love – to that dimension of contemplation where we are 'taken up' into the whole cosmic and gracious flow of prayer, in which we feel that God has taken the initiative, and all we can do is to flow passively with him. This does not mean that it will be full of light and glory. There are times when such contemplative prayer takes us into deeper areas of burdened intercession. But the difference is that whereas previously we were engaged in conflict or confrontation with dark powers with a measure of dependence upon, and faith in, Christ, now he is in control. We have become the instruments of Christ's peace and reconciliation. I am speaking of the deeper reaches of prayer that most of us have only glimpsed.[11] It is the spiritual land of Canaan, the celestial city, the New Jerusalem, and it is also the Paradise regained where Adam once walked with God in contemplative prayer. It is the foretaste of the eternal city, glimpsed here, but entered into fully in the Kingdom of God.

References

1 Acts 13:2.
2 William Barclay, *Testament of Faith* (London: Mowbrays), p. 81.
3 Heb. 4:12.
4 St Antony's story is told in Athanasius' *Life of Antony*, and Augustine's reference to Antony and the account of his own conversion is found in *Confessions*, VIII. 12.
5 Matt. 10:5–13.
6 Quoted by Albert Outler in *John Wesley* (New York: OUP), p. 66.
7 Luke 24:13–45.
8 1 Cor. 11:29.
9 Kallistos Ware, *The Orthodox Way* (London: Mowbrays), p. 149.
10 Isa 55:10, 11.
11 For an elucidation of the deeper reaches of prayer, see 'Mystical Prayer', in *HF*, pp. 177ff.

12: Commitment: A Rule of Life

Challenge, Commitment and Discipline

The Gospel challenges us to a disciplined commitment in a number of ways. We may be stirred emotionally in an evangelistic mission, intellectually by a well-reasoned and convincing argument, or aesthetically by beautiful and well-ordered worship. There are times when the challenge to commitment may come on the Damascus road in a totally unexpected confrontation with God, with the Ethiopian eunuch studying the scroll of the prophet Isaiah, or from within the fasting, praying, believing fellowship of God's people when the voice of the Holy Spirit speaks clearly.[1]

We cannot lay down tracks along which the Holy Spirit must run, for he is sovereignly free to call whom and when he will. But the way of retreat, the setting aside of time and the entering into the desert is a frequent biblical precedent for hearing the word of God. Those who take the business of retreat seriously become aware of their own depths and of the Holy Spirit's interior indwelling, and soon begin to feel and know the responsibility of challenge and evolving vocation.

The problem often is how to live within the creative tension of freedom and discipline – how to translate the free charisms of the Holy Spirit, the soul-stirring appeal, the intellectual quickening and the aesthetic elation into a disciplined response of commitment in daily life. It is one thing to be confronted with the consuming wonder and challenge of the burning bush, but quite another to translate that into risky and courageous action when the threat of persecution and even death is inherent within the situation. It is amazing how easily we can summon valid reasons to our aid in an attempt to evade the solemn responsibility which comes with the vision, as Moses did.[2] But there is no evading of the issue once the Lord calls and confronts the man of God. The prevenient grace which called Moses made it very clear that there was no charismatic call without the attendant grace and gifts to fulfil the vocation to dedicated service. The way was not easy, but neither was it impossible – and in any case, there was no other way. Moses had burned his boats behind him!

Translating Vision into Commitment

The basic response of the believer in conversion and baptism is to embrace the Gospel as one's rule of life. It was St Francis' idea not to follow prevalent monastic patterns which implied the whole panoply and machinery of the mediaeval Church, but simply to follow the Gospel. His first 'rule' was the linking together of gospel-texts which were to guide the life of the friars in a charismatic but disciplined manner. Of course, it is not so easy, for the Gospel is so simple, yet so profound, and he soon found himself both elated and burdened with an increasing number of followers constituting an Order of Friars which was hardly his original intention. In Francis' day there was such enthusiastic response to the lovable God and the supernatural world of Francis' preaching that some people saw the clamouring of people to join him in terms of an epidemic of vocations. 'Too many Minors,' he said, 'ah, but a time will come when the people instead of meeting them everywhere will complain that they are too few.'

A Third Order

There were already the First Order of Friars Minor, and the Second Order of Poor Clares, and in 1216 the people of Cannara wished to leave their homes to follow Christ in Francis' steps. It was then that Francis ordained the Third or Tertiary Order of Franciscans which received canonical status in 1221 in Florence.[3] It was provided with a Rule of Life, and Tertiary Fraternities sprung up consisting of men and women, married and single, constituting the third dimension of Franciscan life.

There are many Christians who are today looking for a viable way to live their Christian lives both personally and corporately, and the making of a retreat often leads them to close relationships with religious orders of different kinds.

Almost all religious orders have a parallel vocation lived in the world associated with their particular Order. This is usually under a definite rule with some direction and fraternity life and obligation. Those who participate may be called Oblates, Associates, Companions or Tertiaries, and constitute not only a support group of prayer and help alongside the Order, but live out the rule of the Order tailored to their needs. This is only one of the many ways of living out the Gospel and of translating the vision practically into a life of commitment and discipline, but it is one which is becoming increasingly productive in terms of Christian discipleship. A letter to the Guestmaster/mistress of any established Order will bring details of such a life within that particular Order, and an explanation of the way we go about it may be of help at this point.

The Franciscan Third Order

The Society of St Francis is a body of Christians within the Anglican tradition who seek to live out the Gospel of Christ in the spirit of St Francis of Assisi. All who participate in this life do so because of a response to an interior vocation – a call of God. The framework and disciplines of such a life enable them to give themselves more fully to the sanctifying work of the Holy Spirit within the love of God. There are particular emphases in the Franciscan tradition, the keynotes of which are humility, love and joy, with the disciplines of prayer, study and work.

The First Order consists of men (The Society of St Francis/SSF) and women (The Community of St Francis/CSF) who live in community under a Rule based on the traditional vows of poverty, chastity (celibacy) and obedience. The Second Order (The Community of St Clare/CSC1) consists of women called to an enclosed life of contemplative prayer with the same vows.

The Third Order (Tertiary Order/TO) consists of men and women, ordained and lay, married and single, between the ages of eighteen and sixty (for admission), who believe that God is calling them to live out a Franciscan vocation in the world. These are the Anglican counterpart today of the original Brothers and Sisters of Penance founded by St Francis referred to above. This life is lived in the midst of secular callings, though lived under rule with a vow of lifelong intention. Normally Tertiaries are communicant members of the Anglican Communion, but there is provision for Christians in good standing in other communions who would be encouraged to be faithful also to their own traditions.

Aspirants to this Tertiary Order, if accepted, would undergo a postulancy of at least six months, keeping an experimental rule before being admitted to the noviciate. The noviciate lasts two years and leads to profession at which Tertiaries commit themselves to Christ within the Order with lifelong intention.

Tertiaries have a counsellor or Spiritual Director who guides them in the life of prayer towards the mature realization of their spiritual potential. The Director is chosen at the time of beginning the postulancy and is approved by the Provincial Chaplain. Every Tertiary draws up a personal Rule of Life with the help of his Director which gives expression within his own particular circumstances to the three Franciscan ways of service – prayer, study and work. The Rule of Life affirms the values of poverty, chastity and obedience adapted for life in the world, and directs the Tertiary towards the Franciscan principles of humility, love and joy.

All postulants and novices are in the care of a Novice Counsellor, who is an experienced Tertiary, and they meet quarterly with a view to spiritual fellowship and development reflected in the Rule, which can be adapted and changed to meet changing circumstances. Members of the Third Order pledge a keeping of the Rule for a year, and this pledge is renewed annually at a Tertiary Gathering. This renewed pledge is the basis of membership and the bond that unites all members of the Order. This is also a safeguard against merely nominal membership and promotes mutual fellowship and love. There is also a dynamic sense of movement and change within the stability of rule and renewal.

Drawing Up a Rule of Life
We cannot guide ourselves. The Holy Spirit is the true interior Director of souls, but within the Body of Christ,

one of the gifts of the risen Christ is the mutuality of help, confession and healing.[4] Many Christians wrongly claim an individualistic hot line to God, but are really only looking for some divine rubber-stamp approval for the affirmation of their own selfish desires. The pattern of St Francis is the pattern of Jesus who said: 'I do always those things which please my Father.'[5] Within the Third Order you may use your Novice Counsellor in terms of spiritual direction, or you may choose your own Spiritual Director. A Rule of Life as Tertiary may run something like this:

1) The Holy Eucharist. This should include Holy Communion on Sundays and Greater Festivals, and may include a weekday Eucharist if possible.

2) Penitence. Regular self-examination and meetings with your Director are commended, which may be followed by Sacramental Confession or personal discussion seeking counsel and advice.

3) Prayer and Meditation. Definite daily periods should be set aside, for the saying of a daily office with its scripture and an evolving discipline of meditation under guidance. The minimum time can be stated in the Rule so that it may be kept without strain.

4) Life-style. This may vary greatly depending upon the age, outlook and temperament of the Tertiary. It should embrace physical exercise, commitment to basic study and spiritual awareness. Matters of fasting and diet, disciplines of tobacco and alcohol and the use of money are all involved. Also included should be 'works of mercy' such as visiting the sick, lonely or imprisoned, and financial help to individuals in need or to some reconciling/helping agency such as Amnesty International, Christian Aid, Tear Fund, etc. The whole matter of tithing and its allocation may be involved here. These are only suggestions to stimulate reflection.

5) Retreat. Tertiaries should make an annual retreat – it may be a Third Order Retreat or a group or private one. If for family or health reasons this is not possible, then a number of Quiet Days should be listed.

6) Study. This is mentioned under life-style, but separate attention should be given to it, depending upon individual capacity and time. Bible-study comes first with commentary aids. It is worth taking advice, reading reviews and sharing in group discussions. Study also involves the Christian learning a little about all the great intellectual disciplines to broaden and deepen one's understanding of God's world.

7) *Simplicity*. The distribution of one's goods was a primary act in early Franciscan life, and the principle of simplicity is relative to one's personal and family responsibilities. The sharing of what is retained must be borne in mind, involving hospitality, provision of transport for others if you have a car, and the using of a bicycle again!

8) *Work*. Quite apart from asking if one's work is compatible with one's Christian profession, it is necessary to allow the Gospel to be expressed in daily work through attitudes, punctuality, honesty and open-hearted humour. The love of God can be manifested in the cleaning of windows, the delivering of milk or the handling of patients.

9) *Obedience*. To see your Spiritual Director at least twice a year should be a matter of obedience. Consideration of obedience involves humility, trust, discipline and humour. Such reflection will also indicate your attitude to authority, responsibility and spontaneity and be a fruitful area for self-evaluation.

10) *Fellowship*. As a Tertiary, it is presumed that worship in your local church and fellowship with other Franciscans is part of your ongoing Christian life. Contact and friendship with wider groups are also encouraged to keep open all the human channels of communication at every level.

All these points can be borne in mind as you write up a possible Rule of Life to be discussed with your Spiritual Director and/or Novice Counsellor. It is better not to set your sights too high, for falling down often means discouragement. If you set your sights lower than your expectations, then it will be an encouragement to feel that the Rule of Life is a help and guide, and can be adjusted accordingly and realistically depending on changing circumstances.

Commitment and Freedom
The hand-out leaflet introducing the Third Order of SSF, says:

We are called to experience the Gospel as the power of God calling for the constant sanctification and renewal of ourselves and of the whole Church.

Our aim is to bear witness to the truth in Jesus, the Son of God, and in this we are inspired by Saint Francis of Assisi and his challenge to a life of humility, love and joy. The life of the Order is rooted in Eucharistic worship and personal prayer and we believe that we are called to service within the Church, enriched and strengthened by periods of withdrawal and retreat.

We bind ourselves to live by a personal Rule of Life and undertake to have a Spiritual Director to help us in our ever-deepening commitment to Jesus. Franciscans believe that prayer, study and work are the three ways of service and in this we aim to encourage and support each other by means of prayer and regular meetings.

Of course, you may feel it totally unnecessary to adopt any Rule of Life which seems to add to the Gospel, and this would be good thinking if any such rule *added* to the Gospel. A Rule of Life is meant to explicate, elucidate and apply Gospel principles to the orbit of one's personal and communal life. Don't labour to keep rules in any legalistic way – the Gospel has delivered us from such legalistic living under law. Freedom, spontaneity and Gospel joy are our inheritance – but this does not lead to *antinomianism* (lawbreaking), but to a disciplined life in which spontaneity and joy are channelled to great good, bearing much fruit in our lives. The vine is pruned in order that it may bring forth fruit, more fruit, and much fruit – and the pruning is the disciplined action of the Holy Spirit.[6]

References

1 Acts 9:1–19; 8:26–40; 13:1–3.
2 See Exodus chapter three. The Vision (vv.1–6); the Challenge (vv.7–10); the Excuses (vv. 11–13).
3 There is a brief but excellent chapter on the Third Order in Omer Englebert, *St Francis of Assisi* (London: Burns & Oates), pp. 229ff.
4 James 5:13–16.

5 See John 4:34; 5:30; 6:38; 8:29, etc.
6 John 15:1–8.

PART III: PILGRIMAGE

A Journey of Experience

13: Deeper into God

The title of the book comes from this chapter because I want to share, at this point, something which I had thought would not easily be shared. Readers of *A Hidden Fire* will recall that I spent my second period of six months' solitude on the high coast at the edge of the Lleyn Peninsula facing the island of Bardsey – a holy enough place anyway. In the context of that tremendous period of light and darkness there were many experiences which are still too deep to share, but there was one which happened in the darkness of Advent on 14th December, the implications of which are still being worked out in my life.

It all began during the night office, which consists of twelve psalms, canticles and two hymns and bible readings. At the reading of the Gospel for the day, the Holy Spirit took hold of me and began such deep and interior teaching that shook me to my foundations, and from which I have not yet recovered, because, as I say, I have not yet fully worked out the implications.

The effect was so powerful that it continued with me through the day, and I was impelled to record it in my spiritual journal, for I knew that I would have to return to it in the months and years ahead. After completing the record, I spent the whole day in the continual and deep awareness of what the Lord was saying. It was an experience something akin to the weight and burden that the prophets felt when the Lord took hold of them and weighed them down with the prophetic word which burned in them, burdened them, churned them with its power. 'For the word of God is living and active, sharper than any two-edged sword, piercing to the division of soul and spirit, of joints and marrow, and discerning the thoughts and intentions of the heart.'[1]

The reverberations of the word of the Lord were such

that I was smitten by it, and it was perhaps the only time during the whole six months that I really needed another human person, though I did not expect anyone to come. I had come to this desolate place of retreat on 10th November, and it was now 14th December. Apart from the first few days no-one had come near, and I was expecting no-one until February when the Guardian of my friary was to visit me. There was no question of my going to seek out anyone, but the pain of my loneliness on that day was such that I had not known during the whole of my first six month period in Dorset.

By about 4.00 p.m. that afternoon, on a bleak and menacing day, with the heave and swell of the sea below and the darkness descending on the peninsula, I was suddenly surprised by a knocking on the door, and found a priest in an overcoat, beret and wellington boots. It was Fr Donald Allchin who was visiting the two or three hermits on the peninsula, and had called to see if I was alright. 'Oh Donald,' I said, 'I'm amazed and so pleased to see you today.' I was overwhelmed by the Lord's timing, and especially in the light of his first words: 'Didn't you receive my letter? I wrote to you about two weeks ago.' I collected my sparse mail from the back of a farm-house at the bottom of Anelog on Friday mornings, and Fr Allchin's letter arrived a few days later, on 18th December!

We were soon sitting together sharing what I had written, for he was the very man I needed at that time in that place, for that particular need. He understood perfectly where I was at that time, and what my needs were. He had himself a similar experience of being strangely and simply taken up by the Holy Spirit into the Lord's will. It was the pattern that the psychiatrist Carl Jung called *synchronicity*, and what the Christian recognizes as God's time. And I was glad.

It was a high point in my experience of solitude, for it was the communication of what solitude meant to John the Baptist, and what persistence in this way could mean for me. It was God's gentle indication that the way was a difficult and lonely way, a way that had to be freely and voluntarily embraced for love's sake. It was a communication to me that could not have taken place at this level any earlier. I had been prepared for it by previous periods of retreat and solitude, and it was an indication of the cost of such discipleship. For John the Baptist the only hope of freedom and fulfilment was 'beyond' the darkness and death of his cell – a leap of faith was fundamental. Only in embracing and holding fast to the response of Jesus could he die in hope and liberty, in spite of the isolation and captivity of his body.

These are the things I had to face in my cell, in my loneliness, in my retreat in solitude. Here follows the description of the whole experience as I wrote it in my journal. It tells its own story, and will shed its own light on your journey.

Your cell will teach you all things

Anelog, Lleyn Peninsula, 14th December: In my time of meditation following the night office this morning, the Gospel reading brought before me most clearly the story that Thomas Merton tells from the Desert Fathers. One of the younger monks could not stay in his cell, but was itching to work, or visit, or do some 'good works' – anything to get away from the solitude of his cell, from himself. And when he confided in the Abba, he was told: 'Go and sit in your cell – your cell will teach you all things.' That is just what I am learning. Part of me is desperate, distracted, vulnerable and frightened. And part of me longs to remain quiet, to face the interior darkness, to learn the loneliness, to let happen what will, for I believe the cell will teach me all things. Let me try to indicate the way it went this morning. . . .

The Gospel was St Luke 7: 19–23. John Baptist is languishing in his prison cell, incarcerated, cut off from light and freedom, surrounded by doubts and fears. He sends two of his disciples to Jesus to ask: 'Are you the Coming One, or are we to look for another?' And in these words are contained the pain and anguish of John's perplexity in the cell from which there will be no reprieve until death. John was a man of destiny – aware from his childhood that he was marked for God. His whole life was an ascetic preparation in the wilderness, and his vision sustained him until he burst in upon the nation of Israel with prophetic power, a new Elijah speaking the word of God after 400 years of silence. So much he understood, and was willing to give himself to God's will insofar as he could see it. He preached the baptism of repentance, the appearance of the Messiah, and bore witness to Jesus as the Lamb of God, the fulfilment of all national and messianic hopes. And he knew that his ministry was to disappear as Jesus began to summon men and women to the Kingdom and to personal discipleship. 'He must increase,' John said, 'but I must decrease.'

As a result of his forthright witness he was imprisoned, and in his cell he reviewed his whole life, the sense of destiny, the meaning of his teaching, the way of Messiah and the person of Jesus. There was so much he did not understand, so much that did not meet his expectation – and something that was clearly wrong. Or was it that he himself was wrong? The very cell seemed to question his sense of direction, his motives, his vision. Incarceration and darkness, loneliness and isolation became interiorized, and the dividing-line between subjective and objective reality became blurred, threatening to disappear. And Jesus himself – who was he? John had believed in some kind of patriotic nationalism in which Messiah would figure as God's spearhead – redemption was national and political as well as spiritual – and some violence was inevitable. But this Jesus? John himself did not, of course, seek or promote violence. There is more likelihood that he had connections with the monastic Essene community near the Dead Sea than any attachment to the nationalistic zealot guerrilla movement. Nevertheless, the Davidic throne was in Jerusalem, and the messianic claim meant political revolution. That's the way it had always been. But in Jesus there was a new dimension – something different, something more radical, more demanding, more perplexing – indeed terrifying. And so he sent two of his disciples to enquire.

When they returned they brought back what must have been, to John, good news and 'other' news. There was revolutionary news of healing, forgiveness and reconciliation, but the other news had to be worked out, puzzled over, understood and accepted in the cell of John's own heart. The true marks of the Messiah, according to Jesus, were works of compassion and reconciliation. The good news of the Kingdom was the supremacy of love, blind receiving sight, lame men walking, lepers being cleansed, the deaf hearing again, the dead coming to life, the poor hearing the Gospel, and evil spirits being cast out by the power of the Holy Spirit. It was left to John to work it out. He had to relate his own powerful preaching ministry and its spiritual renewal to the darkness and suffering in solitude which he now experienced. He had to relate the reconciling compassion of the Messiah to the shadow of suffering which he knew intuitively was falling across the way of Jesus. As he reflected upon his own inspired words: 'Behold the Lamb of God who takes away the sins of the world . . .' he knew that the lamb was the creature of sacrifice, and the vicarious sacrifice was by the shedding of blood.

'Sit in your cell, and your cell will teach you all things . . .' John had lived his life of ascetic preparation, he had embraced his destiny of solitude for the sake of the Kingdom. He had borne faithful witness, braved the authorities, been a lone voice in the desert, accepted the lonely prophetic way of men like Elijah, but there was no chariot of fire to take him home. Here he was, not dwelling in a solitude which he had grown to love, but incarcerated in an isolation which he abhorred. He had been reduced, stripped, exposed before God, and the very foundations of his assumptions, his life and ministry were being eroded and called in question in this cell of loneliness.

It was clear that Messiah was not going to rescue him – at least not in the sense of opening *this* prison, of preaching deliverance to *this* captive. It was also clear that in the message of Jesus lay the meaning, though not a facile solution, to his perplexity. It was somehow that Jesus was other than he had thought, that the way of loving compassion was the politics of the kingdom, that the love of God had to do with the way of solitude and suffering. If these things could become part of John's very soul, then that would be his chariot of fire – the fire of consuming love and compassion. And where would this lead? Well that was not John's business. It could lead to the opening of the prison cell and a further period of ministry and witness – but John somehow knew that the dark shadows of his cell were teaching him something else. It could lead to martyrdom – not the glorious witness of courageous challenge sealed by his blood in the great Maccabean tradition of Israel's glory, but in a private and bloody decapitation on the whim of a dancing girl who had caught Herod's fancy, an ignominious death, planned back in the shadows between her mother and the powers of darkness. John did not know that Tertullian would later say that the blood of the martyrs is the seed of the Church. Nor was he clear about Jesus' meaning when he said that unless a corn of wheat falls into the ground and dies, it abides alone, but if it dies, it bears much fruit. John did not know that here in his cell, the word of Christ would minister to his interior solitude – but he learned that his cell would teach him all things. . . .

And so it is with me this morning. The word of scripture lays hold on me. The Holy Spirit brings the word of Christ to light. The darkness and solitude of my own cell teach me in the silence. And my own perplexity gives way to some glimmering of faith. Things are not turning out as I expected, and I find in myself questionings, doubts and fears.

I am carried back over the days of childhood – the dim sense of the mystery of God from infancy, even before I understood the pattern of the meaning of Jesus' life and words. There is a sense in which I was always a solitary, dwelling in the cell of my own interior solitude. St Francis was right when he said: 'The body is our cell, and the soul is a hermit who stays within the cell, praying to the Lord and meditating upon him.' The pattern of conversion to Christ at twelve years of age and a deepening experience of the Holy Spirit at sixteen years, only clarified the direction of my life which led to ministry within the Church and the world, and called into play all my powers of imagination and creativity dedicated to the service of God. But there were other factors at work, the pattern included light and darkness – there were tensions of personal loneliness within the context of loving and supporting fellowship within the Church. There was the continual strange and mysterious call of solitude while pursuing an active intellectual and caring ministry in Church and university life. There was the occasional blinding glimpse of the divine Love which brought me to tears and perplexity of mind and heart, unable to explain or communicate its interior meaning to myself or to others.

And the world. It has always been clear to me that the love of God is not to be found only in the Church. Indeed, I have often found the spontaneity and immediacy of the divine Love with ordinary people of no particular religious profession, and a sad lack of the same within the professing Church. It has sometimes been a great relief to get away from the pious mouthing of religious jargon and test-case clichés to the simple communication of human values with non-Christian humanists in Amnesty International meetings, or with 'unbelieving' neighbours among whom I have lived.

And public ministry. So much evangelism, lecturing, pastoral care, university chaplaincy, missions, retreats and parish work. What does it all amount to? How much vanity and self-concern has there been, how much projection of a satisfactory image? How much of it is part of the great ego-trip which is becoming more and more obvious to me in the solitude of this cell?

The outcome of this is twofold. Negatively, I am learning that faced with myself alone – with the projected, self-assertive, pseudo-ego that I have identified with for so many years – I am experiencing a threat to my very being. The process which John the Baptist experienced in his cell was one of self-disclosure, of being stripped, exposed, leading to a perplexity that cried out, 'Who am I, Lord, and who are You?' And positively? Well in all this self-denigration, I cannot deny the early awareness, the thread of continued vision, the interior solitary witness which I can only believe is the divine image within the depths of my own being. And the negative stripping of the self-clinging ego is the dying of the old Adam in order that the Christ may be born again within. 'He must increase, but I must decrease.' This means the ancient, biblical and mystical way of purgation, illumination and union with God.

It is both exhilarating and terrifying. And the element

of terror is to the forefront in the darkness this morning, for it is in the context of John in his prison cell, with shadows of incarceration and death all around him. The chariot of fire did not appear in the cell of this greater Elijah, and no such chariot appears to me now. John saw the possibility of such exposure leading to a new dying process which alone would lead him into life. The word of Christ came to him, a word of compassion, reconciliation and assurance – in the midst of his darkness. And that is how it is with me this morning.

The image of the prison cell awakes in me the words of Charles Wesley's hymn:

> Long my imprisoned spirit lay
> Fast bound in sin and nature's night;
> Thine eye diffused a quickening ray,
> I woke – the dungeon flamed with light;
> My chains fell off, my heart was free,
> I rose, went forth, and followed Thee.

I rejoice in the simple, evangelical meaning of this hymn, but like so many of Wesley's hymns it has also to do with the sanctifying and purging experience of dying to the old life, the old ministries, the old self-assertions and confidences. It has to do with the purging fire of the divine Love – but the glimpsing of that conveys the terror indicated in the words, 'it is a fearful thing to fall into the hands of the living God,' for 'our God is a consuming fire' (Heb. 10:31; 12:29).

How strange this is. I have always felt in John the Baptist a frightening, self-denying, world-denying asceticism which I have never felt drawn to – the sort which in negative puritanism and bad catholicism has meant the wearing of hair shirts, flagellation and fear of creative sexuality – all for its own sake. But I have also felt in him the power of conviction, a sense of God-intoxicated enthusiasm, for the sake of the love of God. And so I find this in a much subtler, more profound manner in Jesus himself, 'who for the *joy* that was set before him endured the cross, despising the shame, and is set down at the right hand of God' (Heb. 12:2).

All these things have their application to John in his cell, and to me in mine! I am repelled and strangely drawn, I am scared and exhilarated. I am lonely to the point of desolation, and powerfully held in the solitude of love. These feelings this morning are not sequential but concurrent – they do not follow one another, but are mingled together and serve to drive me into stillness – not to the working out of the insoluable problem of my life and meaning, but to the point of stillness and acceptance which in John's case moved inexorably to an ignominious death, and in my case to that which I cannot at present know.

At this point I look at the text again. It leads to the cross. There is no other way. For John, evidently, his passion lay before him, and in a little while the messianic work of Jesus, healing, forgiveness and reconcilation could not be tolerated by the religious and political authorities. It was a scandal, leading to the scandal of the cross. And that word *scandal* – it is in the text. The last words of Jesus to John are: 'Blessed is he who shall not be *offended* in me.' And the word Luke uses here is the word *skandalizo* – to be scandalized or offended. The same word is used by St Paul in a direct reference to the cross of Jesus: 'We preach Christ crucified, to the Jews a *scandal*, to the Greeks foolishness, but to those who are called, both Jews and Greeks, Christ, the power of God and the wisdom of God.' (I. Cor. 1:23, 24.)

It means that all that is involved in the scandal, the suffering, the darkness and the loneliness of the cross is placed directly before John. Now there is no other way – it is the only way out of the isolation of his incarceration. It is what the cell has made clear to him, and there is no retreat now – only the way forward. And truth to tell, that is what I am afraid of. Every step I take I am aware of this, and up to fairly recently, indeed perhaps still, I have felt that there was a way of escape, retreat, another path. It has been convenient to think that the cross was Jesus' cross, not mine – that he bore the scandal, the curse, the blame, the suffering in order that I may go scot-free. Cheap grace. But I am realizing more and more that he took that way *for* me in order that he may again take that way *in* me. It has to do with my participation in 'the fellowship of his sufferings, being made conformable to his death' (Philippians 3:10).

Yes, I am afraid now – and the words of Jesus, and my reflections do not lessen my fears – but clarify them. Yet with the clarification of my fears there is another and subtle power at work interiorly. It has to do with the Holy Spirit, with the depths of his interior indwelling, and with the ministry of this place, of this solitude, of this cell. And in the darkness and in the silence I sit in my cell – for it teaches me all things.

14: Spiritual Direction

Know Yourself

One of the valuable experiences of making a retreat is that it not only enables you to evaluate your own life-style and place on the Christian pilgrimage, but gives you an insight into the lives and spiritual journeys of others. It soon becomes clear that many retreatants have a kind of life-line which they call *spiritual direction*. And as one observes people who take such direction seriously, it becomes clear that they have certain self-knowledge about where they have been, where they are, and where they are going. I don't mean that they have all the answers – indeed they are usually people who do *not* profess to have pat answers to the world's or the Church's problems. But they are people who are able to live positively with the tensions, conflicts and joys of being a Christian in the kind of world in which we live today.

It is all a matter of coming to a clear understanding of what human life should be about, and what your own particular life should be about. If we are truly following Christ, then we should be on our way to a new humanity, one begotten by the Holy Spirit in the image of Christ. I mean, the more Christian we are, the more human we ought to be. Shortly after I had returned from my first experimental period of six months' solitude, I went over to the camping site of our families' camp in our Dorset friary, and met a young married woman whom I'd not met previously. After a while, she said: 'You are the brother who did six months as a hermit, aren't you?' I grinned at the way she had put it, and said: 'Yes, that's me.' 'Oh,' she replied, 'you're not a bit like I thought you'd be.' 'And what do you mean by that?' I asked. 'Well,' she said, 'I imagined you as ascetic and austere and serious.' 'Well now, was Jesus grim and austere? Did he not love little children and respond to earth and sun and sky?' said I. 'Why yes, of course. . . .' 'So, when I get less and less like him, that's the time to worry,' I responded – and she got the message.

The danger is that if we do not relate to the wider Church, both in fellowship with other Christians in sacramental life, and with someone who can act as a spiritual guide/soul friend, then we shall project an image of a Christian, an evangelist, a preacher, a hermit or whatever, which is subjective and individualistic, and probably eccentric. We need objective, disciplined, corrective counsel within the love and compassion of the Gospel, and we need someone whose gifts and ministry are recognized within the Body of Christ.

A Double Danger

There really is a double danger. First, that we shall be led astray by our own private judgment, puffed up by pride and tempted to self-will. Second, that we shall join ourselves to a sect, group or charismatic person outside the mainstream of the Church, and be led into a hardened attitude of exclusivism, and a dogmatism that does not own the reconciling love and compassion of the Saviour. The word *charismatic* may sound strange in that context, but there are evil charismatics as well as godly ones. There are charisms of Satan as well as charisms of the Holy Spirit, and the gift of discernment in love and truth is needed. That is why we need a Spiritual Director and Guide whose gifts, discernments and ministry are known and owned within the wider Church. Henri Nouwen says this in his book *Reaching Out*:

A careful look at the lives of people for whom prayer was indeed 'the only thing needed' (Luke 10:42) shows that three 'rules' are always observed: a contemplative reading of the Word of God, a silent listening to the voice of God, and a trusting obedience to a spiritual guide. Without the Bible, without silent time and without someone to direct us, finding our own way to God is hard and practically impossible.

It goes without saying that the Christian will give attention to the Bible. But here, too, private judgment must be avoided. 'No scripture is of private interpretation', says the Second Epistle of Peter, and means that the Holy Spirit who inspired the writers must also inspire the readers and interpreters, otherwise scripture will be a dead letter and not of the living Spirit. It must be borne in mind that most of the heretical sects affirm a plenary inspiration of scripture while rejecting the fundamental doctrines of the Christian Faith.

The Desert Fathers we spoke of earlier know of the dangers of isolation, solitude and of private interpretations, and also of the pseudo-prophets and charlatans who went their own heretical ways. Therefore St Basil and the other bishops and teachers in the Church commended the eremitic hermits and the brothers who lived in groups called *sketes* to follow the directions of their spiritual fathers and guides, as a safeguard from self and Satan. 'Do you understand what you read?' asked Philip of the Ethiopian who was reading the scroll of Isaiah in his chariot. 'How can I unless someone guides me?' was the questioning reply.[1]

What Kind of Guide?
When I speak of a Spiritual Director, I am not referring to a kind of legalistic master who directs the passive disciple. But rather in terms of a warm and loving relationship in which direction is sought and discovered in mutual prayer, under the guidance of the Holy Spirit. The words advisor, helper, guide, or as the Celtic tradition has it, soulfriend, could easily be substituted. The latter is a good term because it makes clear the pilgrimage aspect of the relationship upon which both are travelling. There is a spiritual network of guidance and direction which operates with a wonderful gospel freedom, and allows the charisms of the Holy Spirit to be expressed in the Body of Christ to mutual edification. I know of Catholics with Orthodox directors, Anglicans with Catholic directors, Baptists with Anglican and Methodist directors. And so it goes on. The influence of the charismatic movement has done a great deal in this respect, for there has been a mutuality of learning between Catholics and Pentecostals with all shades

between. And often the retreat is the place of intersection and meeting for those of different church backgrounds.

But the important thing in the choice of a Spiritual Guide or Director is his knowledge and experience in theology and the life of prayer. He may be ordained or lay, with formal theological training or not, a full-time church worker or not – it may be a man or a woman. In my own case I have found the canny, intuitive, direct and loving direction of a woman to be appropriate to my own situation. Having said these things, there is a need to understand the mainlines of theological teaching, to be able to discern between good doctrine and heresy, and to have experienced, at least in part, the pilgrimage of prayer. Obviously, it would be needful for me to have recourse to a director who knows the contemplative way, and who is in touch with the hermit tradition. But that would not be necessary in most cases.

The need for such direction is for those who take their pilgrimage seriously, because the path of prayer and spirituality is one which unfolds as you progress. There is more to be encountered, obstacles to be surmounted, valleys and hills to be traversed, corners to be negotiated, evils to be avoided and blessings to be experienced. As well as all this, there is much to be shared, accompanying happenings to be evaluated and questions to be asked and debated. Such a pilgrimage is often dramatic, sometimes tedious and boring (a very necessary part of human life to be accepted), often invaded by joy and hilarity, and occasionally dangerous.

Therefore there is not only need for sharing and direction, but the patience to pray, to wait and to seek in God's own time, for the right man or woman to help you. And before you go off seeking for such, there are some things to be learned and affirmed, and these are as applicable for the making of a retreat as they are for seeking a Spiritual Director or Soul Friend.

First there is the realization that the true Spiritual Director is the Holy Spirit himself. Every Christian has received the anointing of the Spirit in conversion and baptism, and the experienced indwelling of the Spirit is the inheritance of every child of God:

The *anointing* which you received from him abides in you, and you have no need that any one should teach you; as his *anointing* teaches you about everything, and is true, and is no lie, just as it has taught you, abide in him.[2]

The word *anointing* is *chrisma*, from which the word *Christus* (Christ, the anointed One) comes. The apostle Peter uses this word in speaking of the anointed ministry of Jesus:

God *anointed* Jesus of Nazareth with the Holy Spirit and with power . . . He went about doing good and healing all who were oppressed by the devil.[3]

The same dynamic and indwelling Spirit which energized Jesus is given to us:

If you and we belong to Christ, guaranteed as his and *anointed*, it is all God's doing; it is God also who has set his *seal* upon us, and as a *pledge* of what is to come has given the Spirit to dwell in our hearts.[4]

All the italicized words are powerful, full of theological meaning, and are meant to be read, studied, contemplated and applied to our very existence as believers. The Holy Spirit indwells the Church corporately, and EVERY BELIEVER PERSONALLY. This means that the Holy Spirit is the true Spiritual Director, that *he* is the interior guide, imparting the gifts of wisdom and discernment. You see how important those references to anointing are? There are more, if you will take up your bible concordance, tracing the word *anointing* in all its forms in Old and New Testaments. You should not therefore hive off on your own individualistic way, listening only to some interior voice that you alone hear. Nor should you go and join a charismatic, exclusivist sect which pretends to special revelation outside the mainstream of the Church. What you should do is to keep your feet firmly planted within the Church, with the Bible in your hand and the Holy Spirit in your heart. Then you can safely become aware of the voice of the Holy Spirit, for his interior ministry is to be Advocate, Guide and Director.

Therefore, if you have God's Holy Spirit within you, and you open your mind and heart in prayer, guided by scripture within the fellowship of the Church, you already *have* the interior direction you need – *if* you will make space, remain in silent listening, and give your heart to obedience. If you are *not* willing to do this, then no amount of external spiritual direction will be of any use. If you do, then of course you will feel the need for further sharing and probably some guidance, so this brings us to the second matter.

This *chrism* or anointing which you have is the active power of the Holy Spirit within, and therefore sharing of experience within the Body of Christ becomes a necessary joy. You may think of this not only in terms of all manner of fellowship and worship, but also in terms of a relationship with a Spiritual Director or Soul Friend. The latter may be a man or a woman, lay or ordained. Ordination does not necessarily give gifts of discernment which are the primary needs of the person called to lead other souls deeper into prayer. The problem with which we are at present faced is that we seem to think that we need a priest or minister for this ministry, but any believer with the spiritual gifts can undertake it. There is a dearth of such priests, ministers and pastors with the necessary gifts for this particular work, especially as many more people are recognizing their need for such ministry. But the Lord is raising up lay-people who are recognized by their love, wisdom and spiritual maturity – and recognition within the Body of Christ follows. But beware of those who set *themselves* up! My advice then is that you should note carefully what we have said about the interior indwelling of the Holy Spirit, and then pray for the right spiritual Guide or Soul Friend. And in process of time and maturity, it may be that God will call upon you to fulfil such a task for someone else within the fellowship of the Church.

I have said all this within the context of retreats because if you are reading this book you will either already have had experience of retreats or are preparing to make your first retreat, and you will certainly meet people who are involved in the whole network of spiritual direction within the Church catholic. This will help you in the consideration of the kind of person you will need, for obviously, an extremely busy community doctor will not need the same kind of spiritual direction as a hill farmer; and a housewife (or househusband) with three children will not need the same counsel as a contemplative monk. But now let us turn to the theological application of such ministry.

Theology and Prayer: a Great Gulf Fixed?

One constantly reads in theological and pastoral literature from both sides, complaints that there is a gulf between the serious study of theology and the ways of prayer and spiritual guidance. Such a chasm between theology and spirituality does, sadly, exist, and the fault appears to be on both sides. Too often professional theologians are not clearly men of prayer, and those who teach the life of prayer and give spiritual direction do not pursue a serious study of historical and contemporary theology. This is not so much a moral judgment as a professional one! There are faults on both sides, and the problem seems to exist in all the Western churches.

The truth is that the man of prayer is a theologian, for theology is the true, experiential knowledge of God. In the West, one is able to complete a degree in divinity with no experiential knowledge of God, simply as an academic exercise. This is not envisaged in a biblical faith, for in the Bible, knowledge of God is redemptive, and the knowing and loving of God are the two expressions of a unitive relationship. It is true that the devils believe and tremble,[5] but then that is not saving belief, a true knowledge, as the Bible and as faith envisage. The sharing and community element is at the heart of what the Church is. The Orthodox theologian Aleksei Khomiakov puts it this way:

No one is saved alone. He who is saved is saved in the Church as a member of her and in union with all her other members. If anyone believes, he is in the communion of faith; if he loves, he is in the communion of love; if he prays, he is in the communion of prayer.[6]

Monasteries, frairies and retreat houses are ideal places in which productive meetings may take place, in word and silence, between all communions of Christ's Church. And a retreat is the context in which the gulf between theology and prayer can be bridged. If one grows in self-knowledge through spiritual direction, this is also a growth in spiritual understanding. And if one gives one's mind and heart to a study of God in scripture and the writings of true theologians, then one similarly grows in the knowledge of God. Prayer and theology go hand in hand, and any withdrawal from the noise and distractions of the world constitutes retreat. And in the context of such retreat the believer grows theologically and devotionally. The Spiritual Director, by definition, is a man of prayer and theology. He may not have had formal and academic training, but within the Body of Christ he has undergone a discipline of learning and devotion, and is the recipient of particular gifts of the Holy Spirit which enable him to lead and guide other believers in the path of devotion and prayer. He is a man under authority himself, who has known the disciplines of theology, prayer, study and compassion. He is a man who is on pilgrimage in his own life, and has traversed some of the dark and perplexing paths, as well as the way of holiness and glory, and these experiences equip him to help those on a similar pilgrimage.

In saying that such a man may have had no formal training, this is not to despise such training. Indeed, such a man is better for training if his priorities are right. The point I am making is that theological training is not indispensable to a cure of souls. I am grateful to all those academic theologians who have taught me in my years of formal study, in Cardiff, Zurich and Edinburgh. These cities have all been centres of the Reformed Faith, but they have also had sound Catholic theologians who have shared their wisdom and learning. The joyful thing for me is that I have often found that the most perceptive critics of the old style exclusivist 'papist' theology have been Roman Catholic theologians of doctrinal acumen and humour. And they have sometimes been the best apologists for the theology of Martin Luther and Karl Barth. Conversely, those who have been most appreciative of Vatican II Roman

Catholic theology have sometimes been those of the Evangelical or Reformed position. So I am not maintaining that formal theological study is to be deprecated – it is to be pursued with intellectual integrity. But formal theological study is no substitute for the devotion of mind and heart saturated with scripture and with the teaching of the fathers of the Church universal.

Sometimes the theology of prayer and devotion has been called ascetical or mystical theology, but this seems too narrow a perspective, for the whole range of theological endeavour has to do with the life of prayer and devotion. If we are considering the profound mysteries of the doctrines of the Holy Trinity, the Person of Christ, his atoning and reconciling work, or the Person and gifts of the Holy Spirit – they are all mystical theology, and have to do with the healing and formation of the soul in the image of God. The Spiritual Director must be in vital touch with the history and practice of such an experiential theology because it is necessary for the spiritual and intellectual well-being of those he has in his care. There is also the importance of discerning and guarding from doctrinal error, for the mystical and evangelical path is littered with those who have fallen into heresy.[7] Wrong believing and wrong perspective lead to wrong practice.

Direction and the Gifts of the Spirit

The gifts and charisms of the Holy Spirit are listed in Romans 12:4–8, and I Corinthians 12:41–11 and 28–31. These are not exhaustive lists, but are referred to as manifested in the particular church and context to which St Paul addresses himself. The gifts of the Spirit are for all the people of God, though not all gifts for all people. The Spirit himself distributes according to his own sovereign will, and as St Paul says: 'each man has his own gift from God, one has this gift, another that.'[8] The Spiritual Director is presumably a man of discernment and spiritual gifts are available for the ministry to which God has called him. He will not necessarily excel in preaching, healing, administration, or those gifts which are not particularly relevant to his ministry.

The value of his direction and discernment in the context

of retreat ministry is that he will, under God, be able to discern where the retreatant is in his pilgrimage, and give some counsel as to a deepening of present commitment, enabling the retreatant to see the next step or two of the pilgrimage. One cannot expect the retreat conductor to undertake the work of a Spiritual Director or Confessor in one or two interviews, but it will become clear that the serious work of retreat will lead on to proper spiritual direction for the whole of one's Christian life, with someone who may become a particular Soul Friend or Guide.

References

1 Acts 8:31.
2 1 John 2:27.
3 Acts 10:38.
4 1 Cor. 1:21, 22 (NEB).
5 James 2:19.
6 Quoted in Kallistos Ware, *The Orthodox Way* (London: Mowbrays) p. 144.
7 Those interested to pursue the consequences of this statement may look in any theological dictionary under the headings Antinomianism, Apollinarianism, Arianism, Docetism, Millenarianism, Docetism, Pelagianism – and these are just a sample.
8 1 Cor. 7:7.

15: Penitence and Confession

Gospel Forgiveness

The Gospel is good news, and the good news is forgiveness, reconcilation, freedom and relationship. The Gospel has to do with our relationship to God primarily, but immediately overflows in our relationships to others within a reconciling community. But these positive gospel words all imply the dark background of evil and darkness in which the light of the Gospel shines. Forgiveness implies sin and guilt; reconciliation implies estrangement and disruption; freedom implies bondage and incarceration, and relationship implies loneliness and isolation. Even as I write these words, I hear the gospel voice of Charles Wesley sounding in the silence of the monastery:

> Long my imprisoned spirit lay
> Fast bound in sin and nature's night;
> Thine eye diffused a quickening ray –
> I woke, the dungeon flamed with light;
> My chains fell off, my heart was free,
> I rose, went forth, and followed Thee.

There is nothing so sad as to meet a person obsessed by guilt, bound by failure and lacking the assurance of forgiveness and loving acceptance. This is true on a human level, let alone in a man's relationship with God. This week we had a visiting group to the monastery, and I talked to them about St Francis' profound understanding of forgiveness and loving acceptance by God, so that he could, in turn, live such a reconciling life in the world. During the discussion/question time, one of the men in the group said: 'But what if you cannot accept yourself and love yourself as I can't . . .?' And he is not alone. I meet so many people who have a kind of self-hatred, and it is true that unless one can love oneself, then it will not be possible truly to share forgiveness and loving acceptance with those around. This man knew that he could not live Jesus' command to love his neighbour as himself quite simply because he did not love himself.

Of course, the Gospel is not telling us to love that pseudo-self made in the image of Adam, sold under sin, rebelling against God and serving the lower nature. That is the slavery from which we are freed. Through the Gospel we are forgiven and made new so that the true self is being more and more conformed to the image of God, that New Adam, the interior Christ-life which is the manifestation of the new birth. If I know myself to be loved, forgiven and reconciled, then I am liberated by the freedom of Christ to loving service which embraces the whole world, and begins from my deepest self to serve my neighbour. This includes loving my enemies, for it is a stark and challenging word that Jesus speaks when he enjoins us to pray 'Forgive us our sins as we forgive those who sin against us', and then adds: 'For if you forgive men when they sin against you, your heavenly Father will also forgive you. But if you do not forgive men their sins, your Father will not forgive your sins.'

Forgiveness, Reconciliation, Freedom

These gospel words are the hallmark of the Christian life, for if the Christian is not weeping with sorrow and with joy at the same time, he lacks a fundamental understanding of himself and of God. I mean that there is always a consciousness of the sinfulness and frailty of one's own nature and of human nature generally. Only as I realize my own constant need for forgiveness and love will I be able to live in compassion and openness to my fellow. If there is alienation, bitterness and hardness of heart towards my brother and sister, then to say, 'I love God' is simply hypocrisy and deceit. In my first love for Christ at about fifteen years of age I began to learn chapters of the New Testament by heart, and I remember walking and memo-rizing the First Epistle of St John, and being caught up in the glory of the first chapter. It was a mind-blowing experience to *feel* the liberating truth when my Christian experience was young and fresh, but even then I could feel the challenge in these words:

> He who says he is in the light and hates his brother is in the darkness still. He who loves his brother abides in the light, and in it there is no cause for stumbling. But he who hates his brother is in the darkness and walks in the darkness, and does not know where he is going, because the darkness has blinded his eyes.[2]

I have drawn a distinction between the old pseudo-self in the image of the first Adam, filled with the loves and works of the carnal nature, and the new self, born of the Spirit in the image of Christ. The new self is generated and energized by the indwelling Holy Spirit, but it is not easy to see things so starkly black and white in experience. The early Church was full of similar problems to ours, and when I hear people speak of the pristine purity of a monolithic apostolic Church, I look into the New Testament and find that the pattern is diversified in particular churches, all with their own glories and problems. Indeed, the churches which had a multiplicity of spiritual and charismatic gifts seemed to have moral and ethical problems which called forth both the compassion and the rebuke of the apostles. This is true in the Pauline tradition of the Corinthian Church, and also of the Johannine tradition, where again we read:

> If any one says, 'I love God,' and hates his brother, he is a liar; for he who does not love his brother whom he has seen, cannot love God whom he has not seen. And this commandment we have from him, that he who loves God should love his brother also.[3]

John makes it quite clear that the pattern of the New Testament believer is one of an ongoing experience of being forgiven and living in the reconciling freedom which is the result of the indwelling Spirit who continually reproduces the image of Jesus within us. The initiative is with God, and we are both passive recipients and active co-operators with the divine will. The consequence of such a mystical life is a profound contemplative orientation, issuing in loving compassion to humankind. This is envisaged in the Francisan prayer:

> Lord, make me an instrument of Thy peace;
> where there is hatred, let me sow love;
> where there is injury, pardon;
> where there is doubt, faith;
> where there is despair, hope;
> where there is darkness, light;
> and where there is sadness, joy.
>
> O Divine Master, grant that I may not so much seek
>   to be consoled as to console;
> to be understood as to understand;
> to be loved, as to love;
> for it is in giving that we receive,
> it is in pardoning that we are pardoned,
> and it is in dying that we are born to eternal life.

When the disciples clamoured for some sign or badge of their union with Jesus, there was only one sign that he said was valid: 'By this shall all men know that you are my disciples, if you love one another.' The basis of such a Christ-life is a continual openness to the forgiving love of God and a mutual forgiveness between believers.

Confession and Forgiveness: the Basis of Retreat

Mutual confession and continual forgiveness is the basis of our Christian lives, and the making of a retreat is a concentration of the practice and experience of the wholeness of the Christian life. The Epistle of St James is most practical, and it enjoins mutual confession in the words: 'Confess your sins to each other and pray for each other that you may be healed. The prayer of a righteous man is powerful and effective.'

There are a number of ways in which sin is confessed and absolution received, but there is one matter which needs to be emphasized before we go any further, and that is that there is *direct access* of the soul to God, and if we ever speak of any mediation of forgiveness, love or healing through human channels, it is always subject to this, and never compromises the direct confrontation of man and God in redemption. This preserves us from the kind of priestcraft that demands human mediation as a necessity, and interposes Church or sacraments *between* man and God instead of serving as gifts of grace to be means, under the Holy Spirit, for conveying forgiveness, grace or healing to the believer.

We thus affirm the high priestly ministry of Christ as our only Mediator and Advocate,[4] while recognizing the gracious gift of an ordained ministry. Such a ministry of priest or minister is a participation in Christ's priesthood, and may be exercised also by the whole people of God in priestly ministry to the world.

Modes of Confession and Absolution

It is not my purpose to expound the various ways in which confession is made and forgiveness received, but it may be useful to list the common pattern:

1) The individual calling for mercy. This may be in isolation, or from within the context of liturgy and proclamation. It is the cry of the visionary prophet Isaiah, enveloped in unutterable glory: 'Woe is me, for I am a man of unclean lips. . . .'; it is the tax-collector, standing at a distance, lowering his eyes, beating his breast and murmuring: 'God be merciful to me, a sinner'; it is the blind beggar at the Jericho roadside calling repeatedly: 'Jesus, Son of David, have mercy on me.' Sometimes the confession of sin is non-verbal; it is an attitude of helplessness like the poor paralytic let down through the roof by his four friends in desperation, who heard the healing and absolving words: 'Take heart, son, your sins are forgiven . . . take up your mat and go home.' Or it is the believing though somewhat superstitious faith of the ritually unclean woman who touched Jesus' robe for healing. When she was discovered, she came trembling with fear and confession, only to hear his words: 'Daughter, your faith has healed you. Go in peace and be freed from your sufferings.' Again, the enactment of penitence is portrayed in the shocking and tender story of the prostitute who wept upon Jesus' feet, wiped them with her hair, kissed them and poured ointment over them, prophesying intuitively his anointing for burial. Surrounded by religious bigotry and conservatism, she heard the words of Jesus rebuking the pious Pharisees and lovingly addressing her: 'Your sins are forgiven; your faith has saved you; go in peace.' Sometimes, like the Isaiah story, the penitence is evoked by the blinding glory of the revelation of holiness. In Simon Peter's case it began with a homely description of a fruitless fishing expedition, and ends with a sudden and miraculous catch of fish, causing Peter to gasp in astonishment: 'Go away from me, Lord; I am a sinful man.' Jesus' words of assurance indicated a future commission to service: 'Don't be afraid; from now on you will catch men.'[5]

In the case of Saul of Tarsus, the conversion was sudden, the penitence was the lightning-stroke of vision and blindness. The laying-on-of-hands, the healing, the assurance of forgiveness in baptism, and the filling of the Holy Spirit were gifts of the risen Christ mediated by Ananias, the servant of the Lord. This story brings us to the borderland where there was no direct access to the human and historical Jesus, but to the risen Christ 'spirit to spirit' through apostolic word and touch.[6]

2) *Liturgical Confession and Absolution*. Corporate confession and forgiveness within a liturgical context is the second common form. Wherever the priest or minister leads the corporate worship of God's people in confession and pronounces the biblical words of forgiveness, the Holy Spirit is present, confirming repentance and faith in every penitent soul. There are many forms, all using biblical words or conforming closely to scripture. A typical form runs as follows. The priest/minister invites the people to confess their sins with words from the gospels/epistles, and then:

People: Most Merciful Father,
       we confess that we have sinned against you
       in thought, word and deed,
       in what we have done,
       and in what we have left undone.
       We are truly sorry and we humbly repent.
       For the sake of your Son Jesus Christ,

forgive us all that is past
that we may serve you with joy and assurance,
to the glory of your Name. Amen.

Priest: Almighty God have mercy upon you,
forgive and deliver you from all yours sins
through our Lord Jesus Christ,
strengthen you in all goodness,
and by the power of the Holy Spirit
keep you in eternal life. *Amen.*[7]

The authority here is no personal or churchly authority, it is the authority of the Gospel committed to the Church in the words of Jesus: 'I will give you the keys of the kingdom of heaven, and whatever you bind on earth shall be bound in heaven, and whatever you loose on earth shall be loosed in heaven.' The words and actions of the risen Christ to the disciplines elucidate it clearly:

'As the Father has sent me, even so I send you.' And when he had said this he breathed on them, and said to them, 'Receive the Holy Spirit. If you forgive the sins of any, they are forgiven; if you retain the sins of any, they are retained.[8]

3) Private Confession before a Priest/Minister. There are apprehensions in the minds of many evangelical Christians about this form, not without foundation, because of misuse and exaggerated claims in pre-Reformation times. It is not widely known that in the Reformation era it was approved of by Luther and Melanchthon, and later by John Wesley. In the Anglican tradition the 1549 Prayer Book linked confession with comfort and counsel, saying that the confessor should be a discreet and learned priest. Because the Church of England professes to be both Catholic and Reformed, there have always been misunderstandings on both sides, but the practice of personal (rather than private) confession with or before a priest has persisted. John Keble, one of the pioneers of the Catholic revival in the Church of England, saw the regular practice of such confession as of evangelical and catholic importance, while denying any kind of priestcraft, imposing a priest between the soul and God. Free access to God was open to any repentant sinner, and the regular practice of sacramental confession was a gift of the risen Christ for the soul's health.

Fr Michael Hollings has produced an informative and practical book on confession in the Anglican, Roman Catholic, Orthodox and Methodist Churches, entitled *Go in Peace*. In it he says that the practice of confession is at a low ebb generally among Roman Catholics, and yet due to such influences as the liturgical revival, and the Catholic Charismatic Movement, and Protestant communities such as the Taizé Community in France, there is a revival of interest and practice across the denominational board.

It was, in fact, at the Taizé Community that I made my first confession in this way, before one of the brothers. I remember with what apprehension I entered in, and with what relief and joy I emerged from the experience. And from that time I have been enabled to lead others into a firmer trust in God's loving forgiveness by an evangelical use of a simple form of confession.

In many ways, the Anglican communion throughout the world, because of its Catholic and Reformed nature, acts as a 'bridge Church', between the distinctly Catholic and Protestant churches. I am aware of the criticism made by a member of the Church of Scotland, that often neither end of the bridge reaches the ground – but the criticism was made in a humorous and ecumenical context! It is certainly true in my own ministry that I rejoice in fellowship and ministry among Baptist, Catholic, Pentecostal and other varieties of Christians – and my experience is widespread. I am more concerned with leading people to Christ than with making them Anglicans (!), but it may well alleviate apprehensions in both Anglicans and other Christians to know that confession and absolution are rooted in scripture and in the liturgical ordination formulae of the Anglican tradition. At the laying-on-of-hands at the ordination of a priest in *The Book Of Common Prayer*, the bishop says:

Receive the Holy Ghost for the office and work of a priest in the Church of God, now committed unto thee by the imposition of our hands. Whose sins thou dost forgive, they are forgiven; and whose sins thou dost retain, they are retained. And be thou a faithful dispenser of the Word of God and of his Holy Sacraments; In the Name of the Father, and of the Son, and of the Holy Ghost. Amen.

The form for personal confession is found in the section on *The Visitation of the Sick*, before receiving Holy Communion:

Here shall the sick person be moved to make a special confession of his sins, if he feels his conscience troubled with any weighty matter. After which confession, the priest shall absolve him (if he humbly and heartily desire it) after this sort:
Our Lord Jesus Christ who hath left power to his Church to absolve all sinners who truly repent and believe in him, of his great mercy forgive thee thine offences; and by his authority committed to me, I absolve thee from all thy sins, In the Name of the Father, and of the Son, and of the Holy Ghost. Amen.

In the 1980 *Alternative Service Book*, the bishop declares that the priest is called, among other things, 'to call his hearers to repentance, and in Christ's name to absolve, and to declare the forgiveness of sins.' And at the laying-on-of-hands, he prays that the priest may receive grace and power, among other things, 'to absolve and bless in your name.'[9]

It must be quite clear that this kind of personal confession is not *necessary* and *obligatory* upon the Christian – the voluntary and free nature of its offer is part of its joy and usefulness. Most Anglicans do not go regularly to confession, and it is worth remembering that Martin Luther in his *Short Exhortation to Confession* bemoans the fact that because it is free, God's people tend to neglect it. Speaking of such freedom in the Anglican tradition, someone has written, concerning making one's confession:

all may;
none must;
some should;

and then added sadly:

few do!

One of the important factors in such personal confession is that there is a seal of confidence, and the penitent may be completely assured that whatever is spoken between himself and the priest/minister will on no account be repeated elsewhere, or even back to the penitent without him bringing up the matter first. If such a thing happened there would certainly be episcopal discipline! Because of the immense value, great apprehension, and intriguing interest in this form of confession, it will be laid out in detail towards the end of this chapter. But to allay certain fears, it can be confidently said that a Christian may prepare and make his confession with the words:

Just as I am, without one plea
But that thy blood was shed for me,
And that thou bidd'st me come to thee,
O Lamb of God, I come.

Just as I am, thou wilt receive,
Wilt welcome, pardon, cleanse, relieve;
Because thy promise I believe,
O Lamb of God, I come.

4) *Mutual Confession with a Soul Friend.* At this point I can do no better than to recommend an excellent book by Kenneth Leech entitled *Soul Friend.* It is a compendium of Christian spirituality, sympathetic to all traditions, mystical and prophetic, and fully aware of the spiritual and psychological insights of the present day. It makes the point that in the ancient Celtic Church of these islands the custom was of repeated confession and absolution. The absolution was spoken usually by a priest, but at times by a layman. A fifth century monk is quoted: 'God has appointed bishops,

priests and doctors for the instruction of the faithful monks to hear their confessions.'[10]

It is from this tradition that the term 'soul-friend' comes. One of the Celtic sayings was: 'Anyone without a soul-friend is a body without a head', and Kenneth Leech finds in the Christian East an echoing of the Celtic tradition in the words of Theophan the Recluse:

> For the avoidance of error, have someone to advise you
> – a spiritual father or confessor, a brother of like mind;
> and make known to him all that happens to you in the
> work of prayer.[11]

The soul-friend may be ordained or lay, man or woman, but one who is dedicated to God in the Life of prayer, and not necessarily having a formal knowledge of theology, though possessing a saving knowledge of God in Christ. The soul-friend will be a companion on the way, and the counsel and sharing will be mutual. Confession may be between one another, and although the seal of confidence will not be under the firm discipline of ordination (unless the soul-friend is a priest), yet in this more charismatic context, it will reflect the depths of relationship and trust rooted in the Gospel. In the Orthodox tradition it is not thought possible that a man can lead a divine life in accord with the Word of God if he lives without a guide, thus pandering to his own self-will. The *staretz* or elder in the Russian tradition is the soul-friend *par excellence*, and his qualitities include:

a the ability to see into the heart of another, a gift which is the fruit of prayer and asceticism;
b the ability to love others and to make the sufferings of others his own, especially sharing the passion and death of Christ;
c the power to transform the cosmos by the intensity of his love.

To have such a soul-friend is a precious gift of God, and in turn, to become a soul-friend to another is a profound responsibility and joy. And when one thinks of the network of spiritual, mutual friendship, compassion and healing

215

throughout the Church at this level, it gives rise to joy and praise that the risen Christ, by his Holy Spirit, gives such a gift to his people.

5) *Corporate Confession within a Church or State*. There may occur, during times of emergency or war, occasions of churchly or national repentance, in which the whole Church or state humbles itself before God, making confession and restitution, and beseeching God for his mercy and grace. This is the kind of penitential confession represented in the book of Jonah when the city of Nineveh, at the preaching of the prophet, repented in a wholesale manner, thus averting judgment and finding mercy.

Many people may think such corporate acts are things of the past in the present state of moral decline in Church and state, but it may be salutary to reflect upon the catastrophes that are in evidence throughout the world, and of the awesome possibilities of nuclear devastation that may cause the secular mind to reflect upon its ways. Fear of hell and judgment are never the right motive to salvation, but fear of death certainly concentrates the mind! On the one hand, 'the devil is sick – the devil a monk would be' is an ironic statement; but on the other – in the story of the prodigal son, squandering his father's fortune in a wild and abandoned manner, and then losing all in poverty, filth and hunger – the text says:

> when he came to his senses, he said . . . 'I will arise and go to my father, and I will say to him, "Father, I have sinned against heaven and before you; I am no longer worthy to be called your son." '[12]

6) *Priestly and Prophetic Confession on behalf of the Community*. There were times in the prophetic life of Israel and in the apostolic life of the New Testament, when a man or group of prophetic souls have exercised their corporate, priestly ministry within the body in confessing sins and pleading for mercy on behalf of the whole company. The work of the prophet is to *stand before the people* in the name of God; the work of the priest is to *stand before God* on behalf of the people. Both ministries are involved in such penitential confession and reparation. The only plea and

basis for mercy and compassion is the divine grace, for the prophet-priest is supremely Christ himself. Job felt himself responsible, as patriarchal father in the Old Testament, for his own household, and within the Church of Christ this ministry of the priesthood of all believers is misunderstood and greatly neglected.

An examination of the 'call' of some of the prophetic figures of the Old Testament indicate their corporate responsibility in days when corporate awareness was much more basic than in our own individualistic days. Moses, Isaiah, Jeremiah and Ezekiel were such men,[13] and Jesus himself was the representative Son of Man and Suffering Servant of prophetic promise.[14] In the apostolic Church too there was a lively sense of corporate reponsibility for Israel and for the whole world, for it was the Body of Christ.[15]

The Church of God is a holy and royal priesthood, offering spiritual sacrifices to God,[16] and one of the primary functions of priesthood is to feel with profound compassion the infirmities and sins of the people, and to stand in mediating intercession before God on behalf of those who cannot plead for themselves. It is a work of intercession and reconciliation which involves identification with the lost world in its need, confession on its behalf, and an involvement at every level in the work of healing and reconciliation in the community.

If the Church universal lived this confessional and reconciling ministry, and each local parish and congregation exercised its prophetic and priestly function in this way, then the Church would truly become the salt of the earth, and light in the world, reflecting and channelling the priestly and reconciling work of our Great High Priest, Jesus Christ:

Since then we have a great high priest who has passed through the heavens, Jesus, the Son of God, let us hold fast our confession. For we have not a high priest who is unable to sympathise with our weaknesses, but one who in every respect has been tempted as we are, yet without sinning. Let us then with confidence draw near to the throne of grace, that we may receive mercy and find grace to help in time of need.[17]

217

Confession in the Context of a Retreat

As I mentioned earlier, my first confession in the sense of (3) above was made to a brother of the Taizé Community while on retreat at the Taizé monastery in France. It was a memorable experience, and though it was quite clear to me that every repentant sinner had full and free access to God without any human intermediary, I nevertheless felt the need to make such a confession within the time of retreat before a representative of the Church Catholic. I was myself ordained and stood in fraternal relationship to the Taizé brother who was to hear my confession. I remember the trembling repentance that filled my heart, not without a certain apprehension, for this was the first time I had truly opened my heart in confession in quite this manner. I knelt in the small, whitewashed, underground chapel, austere and simple, save for an icon of Christ with a light burning before it. The brother came in, put on a purple stole, the symbol that he was acting not simply as an individual but as a pastor in the Church of Christ, and knelt by my side. He heard my confession in quietness and patience, asked some direct questions, gave a simple penance, shared some counsel, and pronounced the words of absolution. There was the liberating sense of being able to share anything and everything in my heart, knowing that there was the complete secrecy of the seal, by which he was not permitted by his discipline and vows, to divulge any matter which was spoken of within the confession. I had not spoken to him personally before that, nor met him since, but he effectively ministered to me at a deep level, for which I continue to be grateful.

Many people who make a regular retreat do not include such confession, as they have no need to do so, and others invariably do. And there are those who feel they ought, but are apprehensive, either because it has not been part of their tradition, or because they realize how painful it would be for them, although for this reason, necessary. Such people need gently to be helped to see if confidential counselling is appropriate to them as sometimes it is, or if they need also to make a general or particular confession. At this point it would be helpful to summarize the *reasons* for making one's confession in this way:

1) In order to receive a *personal* absolution and assurance of forgiveness when one lacks such assurance.
2) When one has committed a particular act or acts which cannot be spoken of outside the confessional with its seal, or when one is in some physical, psychological or spiritual bondage which needs to be confessed and shared in confidence.
3) In order to 'take stock' of one's spiritual life as a continual and ongoing process on a regular basis with one confessor.
4) As a particular act at some important point in one's life when there is a desire to make a general confession of one's faults, weaknesses, fears and problems in order to initiate a new beginning (e.g. before ordination or marriage, etc.). There may be no desire for a frequent or regular confession following this.
5) In terminal sickness, in preparation for death, when it may be accompanied by the reception of the sacrament of Holy Communion.

Making such a confession saves one falling into despair on the one hand because help and relief from the burden of obsessional guilt can be experienced, and on the other hand can keep one from spiritual pride, in acknowledging constantly the truth about one's life.

I find it humbling and painful to make my confession, and it is certainly humbling to listen to others, but there is also great joy in penitence. To help a person see that he is not alone in his failure or depression, to show the way through faith in Christ to forgiveness and peace, and to pronounce words of forgiveness and assurance is a liberating experience for the penitent and confessor.

How To Do It

Another reason why people may not take advantage of confession is ignorance as to what exactly happens. The actual practice is very simple, and may take place at home or in church – not in a 'confessional' but with the priest/minister seated and the penitent kneeling at the prayer desk or chair beside him (or kneeling together). The confession can be frank, open and honest without any fear of judgmental criticism of a negative kind, or the seal of secrecy being broken. The confessor will listen and not interrupt until the penitent has finished, and then may ask clarifying questions, offer counsel and give penance and absolution. The absolution means that the confessor is simply a channel mediating Christ's forgiveness and love – 'whosoever's sins you remit, they are remitted', and the assurance from scripture is made real and personal to the penitent so that he receives it as something objectively given through the minister of Christ's Church, with Christ's authority.

FORM OF CONFESSION
Pr: = Priest/Minister/Confessor; Pen: = Penitent

Pr: The Lord be in your heart and upon your lips, that you may truly and humbly confess your sins, in the Name of the Father, and of the Son, + and of the Holy Spirit. Amen.

Pen: I confess to Almighty God, before the whole company of heaven, and before you, my father/brother, that I have sinned in thought, word and deed by my own fault. Especially since my last confession (which was . . . ago), I accuse myself of the following:

Confession is made in your own words . . .

For these and all my other sins which I cannot now remember, I ask pardon of God, and of you, father/ brother, penance, advice and absolution.

Pr: (*may ask questions, give some advice, and give an act of penance which may be spiritual reading or an act of reparation or loving service.*)

If we walk in the light as he is in the light, we have fellowship with one another; and the blood of Jesus Christ, his Son, cleanses us from all sin. If we confess our sins, he is faithful and just to forgive us our sins, and to cleanse us from all unrighteousness.

Our Lord Jesus Christ, who has left power to his Church to absolve all sinners who truly repent and believe in him, of his great mercy forgive you your offences: and by his authority committed to me, I absolve you from all your sins. In the Name of the Father, and of the Son, + and of the Holy Spirit. Amen.

May the death and resurrection of our Lord Jesus Christ be the sole basis for the forgiveness of your sins and the gift of eternal life. Amen.
Go in peace, your sins are forgiven; and pray for me who also am a sinner.

For Young People

In our various friaries we often have groups of young people from schools or parishes which constitute the pre-confirmation Quiet Day. The day is treated both seriously and joyously and is a retreat from the school or parish to a friary or monastery for a time before God in quiet, reflection and confession. Sometimes these young people will make the form of confession outlined above, tailored to their needs, and it is most humbling to be the confessor at such times. But there is sometimes another form which may serve as an appropriate ending to this chapter.

One such group of about fifteen young people, together with their priest from Wolverhampton, made such a pre-confirmation retreat at Glasshampton a few weeks ago, and we had a great day together. After meditation (and before tea) we held a *Service of Forgiveness* in which opportunity was given to make confession and receive the forgiveness of the Lord in readiness for Confirmation the next day.

The young people, fellows and girls, gathered in the choir of our small chapel, and a mini-brazier was placed in the centre before the lectern. The previous meditation had included a time of reflection upon their lives and the writing down of their private confession. The form of service included hymns and a reading (the Prodigal Son), with confession together and absolution, after which the written 'confessions' were collected, placed in the brazier, and burned, as a symbol of God remembering our sins against us no more.

After the absolution and burning, there was a time of

silent prayer, and with great joy and gladness we sang together:

> Lord Jesus Christ,
> You have come to us,
> You are one with us,
> Mary's Son;
> Cleansing our souls from all their sin,
> Pouring your love and goodness in,
> Jesus, our love for you we sing,
> Living Lord.

Priest: Go in peace, forgiven Christians, and serve the Lord.
All: In the name of Christ. Amen.

References

1 Matt 6:14f.
2 1 John 2:9–11.
3 1 John 4:20–21.
4 1 Tim. 2:5.
5 Isa 6:5; Luke 18:13, 38, 42; Matt. 9:2, 6; Mark 5:34; Luke 7:48, 50; Luke 5:8, 10.
6 2 Cor. 5:16.
7 For a modern and widely used form, see 'The Order for Holy Communion, Rite A', in *The Alternative Service Book 1980*, pp. 119ff. This is obtainable as a separate booklet.
8 Matt. 16:19; 18:18; John 20:21–23.
9 See 'The Ordering of Priests', and 'The Order for The Visitation of the Sick', in *The Book of Common Prayer* (1662), and 'The Order for the Ordination of Priests', in *The Alternative Service Book 1980*.
10 Kenneth Leech, *Soul Friend* (London: Sheldon Press), p. 197.
11 ibid., p. 34. Pages 44–49 give a brief but important description of the Eastern Orthodox tradition.
12 Luke 15:17–19.
13 Exod. 3:1–20; Isa. 6:1–8; Jer. 1:4–19; Ezek. 2 and 3:1–15.
14 Dan. 7:9, 13, 22; Isa. 53 *passim*.

15 Gal. 3:26–29; Eph 2:11—3:12.
16 1 Pet. 2:5, 9; Heb. 9:11—10:22.
17 Heb. 4:14–16.

16: Pattern for a Seven Day Retreat

A Personal Retreat
The time has come. You have booked into a monastic venue, retreat house or found a cottage or hut in a quiet place. You have all your stores of food and equipment in, and everything is set up for seven days of retreat alone with the Lord. In this chapter I shall map out a pattern timetable for one person, deal with specific needs and attitudes for prayer and meditation, and then give a series of theme outlines together with appropriate scripture and meditations on the particular themes.

The method or technique for centring down is set out in chapter ten, and all that you have learned there applies here. Also the method of using the Bible in meditation. The timetable offered here is only a suggestion, one need not keep slavishly to it, for in solitude there is the possibility of great periods of time for contemplation if the Lord leads in that way. Timetables are made for man, not man for timetables. The possibility of a daily Eucharist may not be realistic, of course, that depends on the circumstances.

1) Timetable

6.30 a.m.	Rise, Ablutions
7.30 a.m.	Holy Eucharist
8.15 a.m.	Breakfast
9.00 a.m.	Centring down
9.30 a.m.	Prayer, Scripture, Meditation: morning theme (this period dealt with under (3))
10.30 a.m.	Coffee/Juice and walk
11.00 a.m.	Creative/manual work (gardening, painting, calligraphy, music, bookbinding etc.)
12.00 noon	Passive surrender (time before God in

	chapel, facing altar, icon, lit candle, or in open air)
1.00 p.m.	Lunch and rest
2.30 p.m.	Walk (either simply open to God or prac-tising awareness meditation or the Jesus Prayer)
4.30 p.m.	Light tea
5.00 p.m.	Centring down
5.30 p.m.	Prayer, Scripture, Meditation: evening theme
7.00 p.m.	Supper
8.00 p.m.	Music (listening or making), walk, dance, write journal
9.30 p.m.	Compline followed by period of resting in God
	Retire

2) Meditation Periods

a. Select the Place. This may be constant, or may vary according to the weather. It may be wise to choose a place indoors from the outset – a chapel, a room or a hut. If you choose the open air, it must be without distraction, and you must be flexible enough to be able to adapt to the inside if the weather becomes inclement.

b. Equipment. Make sure you have everything before you begin – do an inventory. Loose-fitting clothes are best, a track suit is fine, or singlet and shorts in fine weather, but certainly not tight jeans, bras or corsets! Either bare feet or socks, and don't forget to visit the loo before the session. It is impossible to meditate with a full bladder or a full stomach. You will need your Bible, meditation notes or commentary, prayer stool, icon, candle, matches, clock or timer, exercise book and pens, cushion, blanket, and perhaps a small snack if you intend to be apart for a long time. Prepare all your readings now with bookmarks in appropriate places.

c. Settling down. This is preparatory to 'centring'. Find your place, make yourself comfortable, survey your equip-ment, and 'let go' all concerns, fuss and external problems.

Is the 'phone disconnected, and are you away from distractions?

d. Centring. Put into practice the recommended method of chapter ten. Make a simple invocation of the Holy Trinity or of the name of Jesus for protection and trust. Find your correct posture and slowly go through the relaxing procedure. When you are completely relaxed (don't rush it, you have all the time in the world), slowly and quietly begin the breathing exercise – slow and deep and gentle. Then focus your attention (eye, mind and heart) upon the Lord, using the name of Jesus, or a simple gospel word, or the image of the icon or candle before you. You may like to gently repeat the name of Jesus for a little while to help you. Then continue in a relaxed manner, with the gentle rhythmic breathing to enter into rest . . . 'Come to me all who labour and are heavy-laden, and I will give you rest. Take my yoke upon you, and learn from me; for I am gentle and lowly in heart, and you will find rest for your souls. For my yoke is easy, and my burden is light.'[1]

e. Theme. Take up your theme for the meditation, think upon it, let it gently pervade and saturate your thinking processes. Do not strain or concentrate with furrowed brow – there is no struggle or mental push now, just a gentle allowing of the theme to wash over you. When you are ready, take up your Bible and read the appropriate scripture. It is a good practice to read aloud at least some of it. You may like to read straight through, and then go back reading again quietly and pensively, allowing the words to take root in your mind . . . in your heart . . . reflecting gently, even passively, allowing God's Spirit to lead you into your own depths and into the depths of scripture. Some beginners will not find all this easy, while others will take to it almost immediately. However you feel, just persevere, but gently, don't push – move with it.

The time will come when you will not be able to use a commentary or even the hymns/prayers/liturgical material provided, apart from scripture, but if you do use any or all of these, take them up only when you are ready for them. If you do not feel the need for them, then let them lie – the Lord knows what you need, and you will come to know within yourself. You must learn to trust the indwelling Holy Spirit, and discern what to use and when.

Continue in this relaxed, reflective, passive mood, and if you feel you want to write what is being suggested to you in your own heart, you might like to do that now. You could ask these simple questions in relation to the theme and its implications:

What do I hear? (the Lord Illuminates the mind)
What do I feel? (the Lord touches the heart)
What should I do? (the Lord moves the will)

When the time feels right, gently allow yourself to come out of the meditation proper, into the period of response.

f. Response. The writing just mentioned could come under this heading. You have not been saying audible or mental prayers, but you may now like to respond to the Lord in words or song along these lines:

i) Praise and thanksgiving (your own words, a psalm, hymn or chorus).

ii) Words of complaint. The psalms and prophets are full of such – don't be afraid to voice your complaint, your pain, your emptiness, anger, boredom, rebelliousness.

iii) Intercession. You may be moved or even profoundly burdened in intercessory prayer for those in sickness, pain, imprisonment, etc.

iv) Adoration. Times of silence and meditation often give rise to overflowing adoration, the gift of tongues, physical movement and dance.

v) Rest again in silence, and breathe the Holy Spirit of rest.

g. Linger. Affirm that all life, light and love come from the creative Spirit of God. Perhaps you will be brought to tears, to joy, or just to a quiet spirit where all images disappear. Allow a spirit of gratitude to well up within you, and conclude the time with a commendation of yourself and of the whole creation to God, Father, Son and Holy Spirit.

Different days will bring different experiences, don't demand any particular experience, and don't be surprised if the Lord turns the tables on you. If you are exploring a week of solitude for the first time it would be well to have a lifeline to someone if you find yourself out of your depth spiritually or even physically. Solitude is beautiful, but also dangerous.

3) Daily Themes

The daily themes for the seven days contain, as well as the main Gospel reading of the theme proper, supporting Old Testament and Epistle readings, and two hymns for devotional reflection if needed. The hymns are taken from the Anglican *English Hymnal*, which is a fine objective type book in the Catholic tradition, and from *Hymns of Faith*, published by Scripture Union, in the Evangelical tradition. For me, it is a basic, theologically important matter that most of the hymns chosen are to be found in both these books. The collects are written for the themes, though all readings and collects may be found in the *Alternative Service Book*, page numbers are given, and this saves leafing to and fro in a Bible and prayer book, especially at a time when heart and mind are lifted to God in quietness and meditation. The actual textual references are given for convenience. Abbreviations *EH*, *HF* and *ASB* will be understood from the above paragraph.

You may find it necessary only to use the gospel reading on the theme, but the rest of the material is supportive and useful if you develop the theme in your meditation or later study.

Invocation of the Holy Trinity:
God my Father,
    You have always loved me; let me rest in your love;
Jesus, my Saviour,
    You lived, died and rose for me; cleanse me in your
    precious blood;
Holy Spirit, my Counsellor and Guide,
    Continue your work of grace in my life today.

Day 1: Morning
Theme: The Incarnation Of the Eternal Word in Jesus
Collect: All praise to you, heavenly Father,

For you gave your incarnate Son to be our Saviour,
to take our nature upon him in becoming man;
may we share in your divinity
as he shared in our humanity,
who lives and reigns with you and the Holy Spirit,
one God, now and for ever. Amen.
    or *ASB* 443

Old Testament:	Isaiah 9: 2, 6–7; *ASB* 444
Epistle:	Hebrews 1: 1–5; *ASB* 446
Gospel:	John 1: 1–14; *ASB* 449
Hymns:	*ÉH* 338/*HF* 115: At the Name of Jesus
	EH 29: The Great God of Heaven
	HF 116: Thou art the Everlasting Word

Day 1: Evening
Theme: The Infancy and Boyhood of Jesus
Collect: Heavenly Father,
Through the days of infancy and childhood
you guided and protected your dear Son,
preparing body, mind and spirit
for his healing and redeeming vocation;
May we place a childlike trust in you,
and so be led by your Holy Spirit
to fulfil your will and glorify your name,
    through Jesus Christ our Lord. . . .
    or *ASB* 450

OT:	1 Samuel 1: 20-end; *ASB* 452
Ep:	Romans 12: 1–8; *ASB* 452
Gosp:	Luke 2: 22–40; *ASB* 453
Hymns:	*EH* 46: In Stature Grows the Heavenly Child
	HF 172: The Son of God His Glory Hides

Day 2: Morning
Theme: The Baptism of Jesus
Collect: Almighty God, our Father,

Your dear Son was baptized for us in the river Jordan,
and was empowered by the Holy Spirit for service;
May we be identified with him in his dedication,
that through his baptism of death and resurrection
we may be brought to your eternal glory,
  through Jesus Christ our Lord. . . .
  or *ASB* 463

OT:	1 Samuel 16: 1–13; *ASB* 463
Ep:	Acts 10: 34–38; *ASB* 464
Gosp:	Matthew 3: 13-end; *ASB* 464
Hymns:	*EH* 6/*HF* 138: Hark the Glad Sound
	EH 459/*HF* 170: O Love how Deep, how Broad, how High

Day 2: Evening
Theme: The Temptation of Jesus
Collect: God our Father,
Filled with the power of the Holy Spirit
your dear Son Jesus was led into the wilderness
to be tempted by the devil;
In the dark places of our lives
sustain us by your word and Spirit,
and bring us out of temptation
that we may serve you with a joyful heart,
  through Jesus Christ our Lord. . . .
  or *ASB* 504

OT:	Genesis 2: 7–9; 3: 1–7; *ASB* 504f.
Ep:	Hebrews 2: 14-end; *ASB* 505
Gosp:	Matthew 4: 1–11; *ASB* 505f.
Hymns:	*EH* 471/*HF* 176: Praise to the Holiest in the Height
	EH 414/*HF* 286: Jesu, Lover of my Soul

Day 3: Morning
Theme: Jesus the Master
Collect: Our Heavenly Father and Guide,
The Lord Jesus called disciples to follow him,

to learn, to serve and to give themselves to him;
As we hear his call and seek to follow,
may we be filled by your grace and forgiving love
in order that we may lead others to follow too,
and be brought at last to your eternal kingdom,
    through Jesus Christ our Lord. . . .
    or *ASB* 467

OT:	1 Samuel 3: 1–10; *ASB* 469
Ep:	Acts 26: 1, 9–20; *ASB* 467f.
Gosp:	John 1: 35-end; *ASB* 470f.
Hymns:	*EH* 205/*HF* 481: Jesus Calls Us
	EH 582/*HF* 476: Take my Life

Day 3: Evening
Theme: Jesus the Teacher
Collect: We give you thanks, our Father,
for the simplicity and clarity of Jesus' teaching;
so simple that a child can understand,
so profound that there is always more to learn;
give us humble and contrite hearts,
to hear, to understand, and to obey,
    through Jesus Christ our Lord. . . .
    or *ASB* 713

OT:	Leviticus 19: 9–18; *ASB* 713f.
Ep:	Romans 12: 9-end; *ASB* 714
Gosp:	Luke 10: 25–37; *ASB* 714f.
Hymns:	*EH* 343/*HF* 490: O Thou Who Camest from Above
	EH 574/*HF* 299: I Heard the Voice of Jesus Say

Day 4: Morning
Theme: Jesus The Healer
Collect: We offer thanks, our Father
for the healing ministry of your dear Son,
for his miracles of healing upon earth,
and for his healing presence in our hearts;
may we, anointed by the Holy Spirit,
radiate the healing power of Jesus

so that others may be drawn to his love,
   through Jesus Christ our Lord. . . .
   ASB 929

OT: 1 Kings 17: 13-end; *ASB* 929
Ep: James 5: 13–16; *ASB* 930
Gosp: Matthew 8: 5–17; *ASB* 931

Hymns: *EH* 446/*HF* 1: O For a Thousand
                          Tongues
                          EH 526/*HF* 174: Thine Arm, O
                          Lord

Day 4: Evening
Theme: Jesus the Healer
Collect: God, the Father of all,
Your compassion and healing power
was manifested in the ministry of Jesus;
let that healing power be revealed again
in the lives and ministry of your people,
that the world may feel the compassion of your heart,
   through Jesus Christ our Lord. . . .
   or *ASB* 490

OT: Deuteronomy 8: 11-end; *ASB* 650
Ep: Acts 4: 8–12; *ASB* 651
Gosp: Luke 8: 41-end; *ASB* 651f.

Hymns: *EH* 470/*HF* 9: Praise, my Soul
                          EH 266/*HF* 93: At Even, Ere the
                          Sun was Set

Day 5: Morning
Themes: Jesus the Liberator
Collect: Almighty God and Father,
Our world is full of darkness,
of anguish and of suffering;
may the healing and liberating power of Jesus
set free those who live in bondage and captivity,
thus manifesting your love,
and glorifying your name,
   through Jesus Christ our Lord. . . .
   or *ASB* 490

OT:	1 Kings 5: 1–14; *ASB* 492
Ep:	2 Corinthians 12: 1–10; *ASB* 493
Gosp:	Mark 2: 1–12; *ASB* 491
Hymns:	*EH* 408/*HF* 436: Immortal Love
	EH 316/*HF* 283: Just as I Am

Day 5: Evening
Theme: Jesus Transfigured
Collect: Upon the holy mountain, O Lord,
your dear Son was transfigured in glory,
and clothed in the Holy Spirit;
come now and transfigure our lives,
that we may hear your heavenly word,
gaze upon the glory of Jesus,
and walk in the power of your Holy Spirit,
through Jesus Christ our Lord. . . .
or *ASB* 792

OT:	Exodus 34: 29-end; *ASB* 792
Ep:	2 Corinthians 3: 4-end; *ASB* 792f.
Gosp:	Luke 9: 28–36; *ASB* 793f.
Hymns:	*EH* 258/*HF* 114: Christ Whose Glory
	EH 235: 'Tis Good, Lord, To Be Here

Day 6: Morning
Theme: Jesus the Saviour
Collect: God our Heavenly Father, as we enter into the mystery of the passion of your dear Son, our Saviour, help us to become aware of his compassion, and to feel his sufferings for our sins, that we may be partakers of his glory, through Jesus Christ our Lord. . . . or *ASB* 539.

OT:	Isaiah 49:1–6; *ASB* 539
Ep:	Hebrews 4:12–end; *ASB* 506
Gosp:	Luke 22:39–65; *ASB* 543
Hymns:	*EH* 70/*HF*177: Ah, Holy Jesus
	EH 300/*HF* 529: According to Thy

Gracious Word

Day 6: Evening
Theme: Jesus the Saviour
Collect: God our Father,
Our Lord Jesus Christ endured the cross,
despising the shame,
because of the joy that was set before him;
In all our darkness and loneliness
help us to affirm your loving presence
and the victory of the resurrection,
   through Jesus Christ our Lord. . . .
   or *ASB* 545

OT:	Isaiah 50: 4–9; *ASB* 545f.
Ep:	1 Peter 2: 19-end; *ASB* 546
Gosp:	Luke 23: 1–49; *ASB* 549ff.
Hymns:	*EH* 102/*HF* 182: O Sacred Head
	EH 107/*HF* 281: When I Survey

Day 7: Morning
Theme: Jesus the Risen Lord
Collect: Lord God, Creator, Sustainer and Redeemer,
We give you thanks and praise
that Jesus Christ is the Sovereign Lord of life and death;
Because he suffered, died, and is risen
we have firm hope and abounding faith;
Keep us ever in your love,
And fulfil in us your perfect will,
   through Jesus Christ our Lord. . . .
   or *ASB* 573

OT:	Exodus 14: 15–22; *ASB* 575
Ep:	Revelation 1: 10–18; *ASB* 576
Gosp:	John 20:1–18; ASB 578.
Hymns:	*EH* 625/*HF* 200: The Strife is O'er
	EH 147/*HF* 206: The Head That Once

Day 7: Evening
Theme: Jesus' Presence and Promise

Collect: God and Father of our Lord Jesus Christ,
Through the eternal Spirit
Jesus offered himself to you in life and death,
And by that same Spirit
rose victorious over the grave;
He is alive for evermore,
and has the keys of hell and of death;
We rejoice in his victory,
And pray that his glory may be reflected in our lives,
    through Jesus Christ our Lord. . . .
    or *ASB* 630

OT:	2 Kings 2: 1–15; *ASB* 632
Ep:	Ephesians 4: 1–13; *ASB* 633
Gosp:	Luke 24: 45-end; *ASB* 634
Hymns:	*EH* 127/*HF* 197: Alleluia, Alleluia
	EH 145/*HF* 203: See the Conqueror

Acclamation to the Holy Trinity:
To God the Father who loved us from the foundation of the world,
To God the Son who redeemed us by the shedding of his blood,
To God the Holy Spirit who indwells the hearts of his faithful people,
To the one true God be all love, glory and praise for ever.
AMEN.

References
1 Matthew 11: 28–30
2 An entirely new edition of *EH* has just been published in which nearly all the hymns listed above are included, with others on the same themes: *The New English Hymnal* (Norwich: The Canterbury Press).

Epilogue: Retreat and Return

Throughout this book I have been aware of a threefold concern. First, that the desire and experience of retreat must have to do with personal experience of God; second, that the roots of such an experience are found within the scriptural soil of the Old and New Testaments; third, that the whole adventure is within the great tradition of the Fathers of the Faith.[1]

My stance has been one of recommending that retreats be taken up into one's personal and communal spirituality, and that the Christian pilgrimage be seen in the light of a kind of retreat and return in the life of prayer. But by implication I have gone much further, for I would prefer to think of the work of retreat not as an optional extra, but as a biblical pattern of patriarchs, prophets and apostles, and practised continually by Christ himself.

My own experience of retreat and return has been powerfully positive, for although I have twice been into the wilderness for six months, I have come back with a deeper compassion, clearer understanding and wider horizons. I believe that I am not only a humbler Christian (though that's not really for me to say!), but also a better human being. These two things are inseparable. The chapter on humour is not misplaced, for my 'sense' of humour, human and divine, is keener even in the face of the horrific possibilities of cosmic catastrophe. Thus I believe I live more in the light of eternity, and yet am more committed to the alleviation of human suffering in all its forms. This is especially the case in terms of the arms race and world peace.

Retreat: An Ongoing Experience
Once the practice of making a retreat has become part of your spirituality, it will become an essential part. It is not

an esoteric practice for elite Christians, but an essential ingredient in the following of Christ. One of the profitable books on retreat venues (listing over 200), is entitled *Out of This world*. It may be a fetching title, but it can give a wrong impression. It is 'in Christ' that the retreat experience operates, and whether there is exposure to ecstasy or darkness, it is very much *in this world*. The Incarnation meant that Jesus' feet were firmly planted in the soil of our human experience, and God becoming man is the pattern of spirituality for our time.

Having said that, I have found that it is the experience of retreat in solitude and silence that has made me more aware than ever before of the precious joy and value of being simply human; yet also of the reality of life in the spirit which is earthed in our humanity but reaches out into areas of the transcendent and the eternal.

Ultimately we are bound for the Kingdom of God. That is not to say that it does not begin here and now – it does! But its consummation and fulfilment is what the theologians call *eschatological*. It affirms the reality of immortality and union with God. These are not two lives but one. Eternal life, *post mortem*, is a glorious and fuller continuation in the nearer presence of God, flowing out into an eternal and increasing experience of union with the Holy Trinity. The experience of retreat, of wilderness, of solitude, of silence, serves to prepare one for death with a new compassion, a new awareness, and a new joy.

And the Return

Does all this mean that you return to ordinary living after retreat imbued with holiness, filled with joyful hope and baptized with love? Well it may! But more likely you will find, as Jesus did, that the baptism in the Holy Spirit at Jordan's wilderness is followed by temptation; that the high glory of Transfiguration is followed by the cry of human need and suffering in the valley. There is no place for a parade of piety, a sermon on transcendence or an otherworldly aloofness from the sweat and dirt of daily living.

But whatever meets you on your return (and be warned of the negative possibilities, for the devil will be ready for you), you will have learned a little more about God, a little more about our common humanity, and a little more about yourself. And that will stand you in good stead for the Christian life to be lived out in your daily occupations.

There is a great deal more to be learned about retreats – but it is to be acquired only by experience. This book may have indicated various dimensions, possibilities and implications, but you now have to translate these into concrete action.

At the time of writing there is a proposal for me to enter yet a third period of six months' retreat in solitude, as a result of which we shall put our heads together to see what the Lord is saying about the future of such a vocation.

The very fact of this gives me amazing joy and hope, not without much apprehension. The infinite possibilities of joy in God are overwhelming – and the interior knowledge that I can only respond if it is in terms of God's *call*, of *vocation* – these things provoke longing, yearning, pain and love in my heart.

From beginning to end it is of free, unmerited, intoxicating grace! And while I continue to spend energy, time and talents in the service of my brothers and sisters in the Church and the world, I long to behold the face of God in glory, and to dwell in intimate and ultimate union with him. This is the experience of present salvation and eternal yearning that I have sought to share in this book, and if it serves to stimulate others to make the pilgrimage of retreat their own, it will cause me much joy.

I have been intending to end this book with the last stanza of the hymn with which I began:

Then, fresh from converse with your Lord, return
    And work till daylight softens into even;
The brief hours are not lost in which you learn
    More of your Master and His rest in heaven.

but one of the lesser-known Wesley hymns has been singing itself in my heart, reiterating that basic desire and longing from which all my human concerns and compassions flow. If I do not end with it, I shall not be true to my basic orientation. So here it is:

God only knows the love of God:
O that it now were shed abroad
   In this poor stony heart!
For love I sigh, for love I pine;
This only portion, Lord, be mine,
   Be mine this better part.[2]

References

1 Here, as at the beginning, I indicate that the language is generic and not simply masculine or exclusive.

2 The hymn begins: *O Love Divine, how Sweet Thou art*, and is best set to the tune *Pembroke*. The references to Mary the contemplative in the hymn are based on Mary of Bethany in Luke 10:38–42.